"Brother Keith, your latest book (*Letters from the Front*) has refreshed my spirit, and I wish you good success in all your endeavors for the kingdom of God."

—Dr. Myles E. Munroe
President/Senior Pastor
Bahamas Faith Ministries International
Nassau, Bahamas

Brianna
the Beautiful.
You are such
a wonderful &
loving friend.
we love you.
Keith &
Bonnie

Letters

from the front

Letters

from the front

by Keith Shealy

TATE PUBLISHING & ENTERPRISES

Published by Tate Publishing & Enterprises, LLC
127 E. Trade Center Terrace | Mustang, Oklahoma 73064 USA
1.888.361.9473 | www.tatepublishing.com

Tate Publishing is committed to excellence in the publishing industry. The company reflects the philosophy established by the founders, based on Psalm 68:11,
"The Lord gave the word and great was the company of those who published it."

Book design copyright © 2008 by Tate Publishing, LLC. All rights reserved.
Cover design by Janae J. Glass
Interior design by Kandi Evans

Published in the United States of America

ISBN:978-1-60462-810-4
1. Christian Living: Spiritual Growth: Spiritual Warfare/Spiritual Formation
2. Inspiration: Motivational: General
08.04.03

Eagle Project Communications
Post Office Box 1152
Yorktown, Virginia 23692
www.towardthemark.com

"But they that wait upon the Lord shall renew their strength; they shall mount up with wings as eagles; they shall run, and not be weary; and they shall walk, and not faint."

Isaiah 40:31

Our goal for the Eagle Project is to supply believers of all ages with a practical teaching of God's Word that will encourage, strengthen, equip, and impart the kind of faith in the Lord that will allow us to reach new heights in our service to both God and His people.

Dedication

This collection of letters is dedicated to all who are soldiers in the army of God. To all who have fought and are fighting the good fight of faith in fields both at home and abroad. To those who for the sake of the Kingdom of God suffer all manner of tribulation and loss for the establishment of God's perfect will and purpose on the earth. To those who willingly invest everything dear to them to see the name of Jesus Christ lifted up in the eyes and hearts of everyone they encounter. For this we both honor and salute every one of you!

Contents

Introduction
13

Sin Makes Ya Stewpit
17

The Crisis of Eroding Integrity
27

Too Quick to Compromise
35

Please...Stop Stinkin'
47

Let It Go
55

Into the Secret Place
67

The Cart's before the Horse
79

The Fruit's on the End of the Limb
89

The Rarest of All Breeds!
101

Three Keys to God-Pleasing Faith
115

Understanding the Fear of the Lord
131

Give to Give
151

The Prayer of Salvation
165

Welcome Home!
167

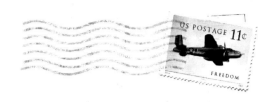

Introduction

All successful warriors have these two things in common: they know their assignment and are well prepared for anything that they may encounter. Knowing your attacker's motives, weaponry, and capabilities will always give you the advantage or upper hand in any battle. Perfect preparation is a soldier's greatest weapon and ally in the field of battle! For example, I really enjoy watching the movie *Patton* starring George C. Scott. For me it is one of those movies that just never seems to get old. In the film, George C. Scott plays the role of the famous World War II American General, George S. Patton. There is one scene in particular that really grabbed my attention, concerning being "perfectly prepared" for battle. In the film, Patton and the II Corps were preparing to enter into a fierce tank battle with the famed German General, Erwin Rommel, nicknamed "The Desert Fox." Several scenes before this great clash was to take place, the writers of the script made it a point to show that General Patton had been studying a book that Field Marshall Rommel had written on tank warfare. In the next scene, as Patton's men are almost effortlessly forcing a division of Rommel's tanks and troops to retreat, the camera pans from its shot of the battlefield to a close-up of Patton's face as he yells with a loud voice, "Rommel, I read your book!" Historians say that the real General Patton was an avid student of history's great warriors and was by far one of the most well-read and best-prepared generals of the war. Patton's determination to stay focused on his objective combined with his knowledge of his enemy's tactics made him one of the most successful and decorated heroes of World War II.

In order to become a successful soldier in God's army you must become perfectly prepared. It is of the utmost importance that first, you know God and His Word intimately; second, you are focused intently on fulfilling His plan and purpose for your life; and third, like General Patton, you are familiar with your enemies' tactics as well as the arsenal that is available to you as a believer in Christ. You must always remember that mere preparation does not ensure maximum effectiveness where the things of God are concerned. Only perfect preparation will ensure maximum effectiveness! For example, the Word of God does not say that those who merely seek God will be rewarded by Him. The Word says that, "God is a rewarder of them that diligently seek Him!" (See Hebrews 11:6.) You must give your all!

It is also of the utmost importance that you understand that when Jesus reached his goal at Calvary, the war was won! Contrary to popular belief, neither the

Jews, the Romans, nor the devil killed Jesus. Jesus successfully finished exactly what He came to earth to do! The word "kill" means to "terminate before completion." Jesus was not killed, He "finished"! When Jesus uttered the words "it is finished," His mission here on earth was fulfilled. As the supreme General of the soon-coming host of heaven, Jesus came to earth in the form of a man and fought His way to the cross; no one had to drag Him there!

> Looking unto Jesus the author and finisher of our faith; who for the joy that was set before him endured the cross, despising the shame, and is set down at the right hand of the throne of God.
>
> Hebrews 12:2

As a result, those who have an intimate relationship with Him all share in His victory at Calvary, and the truth be known, Satan and his hordes do not like it one bit. This is one reason why even though Jesus has won the war, you still deal with various battles in life. It is my prayer and the prayers of the partners of Toward the Mark that these letters will encourage, educate, and equip you to emerge victorious both in your walk with God as well as in any and all of the battles that you encounter along the way.

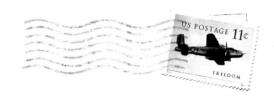

Sin Makes Ya Stewpit

Anyone who knows me can probably tell you that one of my favorite television networks is Animal Planet and that my favorite show on that channel was the Crocodile Hunter. Who of us who has seen the show has not been impressed and thoroughly entertained by the skillful antics of the show's late host, Steve Irwin? His unparalleled knowledge of animals was fascinating, but it was his lifelong experience with reptiles, namely snakes, that I would like to bring to your attention. If you have watched the show, you have likely seen Steve, on many occasions, handling the most dangerous and highly venomous snakes in the world. And if there is one thing that he has made abundantly clear to his viewers it is the crippling and even deadly effects that snake venom can and does have on the human body. Extreme caution must be exercised when anyone is ever around one of these slithery critters! As a matter of fact, the best thing you can do if ever confronted by a venomous snake is to turn and run away immediately!

The majority of all snake venom falls in the category of poisons that the toxicology community refers to as hematoxins and neurotoxins. A hematoxin is a two-part word with "hema" meaning "blood" and "toxin" meaning a "toxic poison." A hematoxin is a poison that causes the blood to coagulate or thicken on contact. The word "neurotoxin" is also made up of two words with "neuro" meaning "the nervous system" and "toxin" meaning a "toxic poison." Simply put, when a person is envenomed by one of these fanged creatures, both their circulatory and nervous systems become brutally traumatized. Shortly thereafter, muscle tissue begins to dissolve, and vital organs of the body begin to fail resulting in numbness, blurred vision, impaired judgment, a decreased sense of hearing, excruciating pain, eventual unconsciousness, and if not treated in time, permanent paralysis or certain death. Like sin, death actually begins at the point of envenomization.

If there could ever be a clear parallel drawn between natural and spiritual things, it's here. For example, in the spiritual sense, sin, like the snake's venom in our story, inflicts upon the souls of its victims trauma that also results in numbness, blurred vision, impaired judgment, drowsiness, a dulled sense of hearing, excruciating pain, eventual unconsciousness, permanent paralysis and ultimate death if not dealt with in time. As someone who has suffered through the crippling effects of sin as well as the painful traumas associated with being bitten by a venomous snake, I have found this to be all too accurate. James, knowing full well the toxic effects of sin, teaches,

Blessed is the man that endureth temptation: for when he is tried, he shall receive the crown of life, which the Lord hath promised to them that love him. Let no man say when he is tempted, I am tempted of God: for God cannot be tempted with evil, neither tempteth he any man: But every man is tempted, when he is drawn away of his own lust, and enticed. Then when lust hath conceived, it bringeth forth sin: and sin, when it is finished, bringeth forth death.

James 1:12–15

The most widely publicized example in the Bible of someone yielding to the temptation of a certain serpent's allure would be Eve in the third chapter of Genesis.

Now the serpent was more subtle than any beast of the field which the LORD God had made. And he said unto the woman, Yea, hath God said, Ye shall not eat of every tree of the garden? And the woman said unto the serpent, We may eat of the fruit of the trees of the garden: But of the fruit of the tree which is in the midst of the garden, God hath said, Ye shall not eat of it, neither shall ye touch it, lest ye die. And the serpent said unto the woman, Ye shall not surely die: For God doth know that in the day ye eat thereof, then your eyes shall be opened, and ye shall be as gods, knowing good and evil. And when the woman saw that the tree was good for food, and that it was pleasant to the eyes, and a tree to be desired to make one wise, she took of

the fruit thereof, and did eat, and gave also unto her
husband with her; and he did eat.

Genesis 3:1–6

This chapter then tells us of the amazing and heartbreaking shift that took place in Adam and Eve's circumstances as a result of their yielding to temptation
and therefore allowing sin's entrance into their lives.
As a result of what I call "sin'venomation," they experienced the most terrifying and horrible death known
to all of mankind, separation from God. One moment
they were in a close, intimate, love relationship with
Him enjoying all of His abundant riches, and the next
they found themselves in utter poverty. Talk about a
"riches to rags" story. Not only did their disobedience
affect them, but it has also affected every generation
that has followed. Don't be deceived. Rarely if ever does
the act of sin only affect the life of the one who has
committed it. Satan enjoys immensely the thought of
being able to kill two or more birds with one stone, so
to speak!

Solomon in the book of Ecclesiastes warns of the
terrible consequences of yielding to temptation when
he said, "He that diggeth a pit shall fall into it; and
whoso breaketh an hedge, a serpent shall bite him"
(Ecclesiastes 10:8). When addressing the dangers of
entertaining temptation, a pastor friend of mine says,
"If you mess around the ole creek bank long enough
you'll eventually slip and fall in." What did Solomon
mean by the word "hedge"? The Webster's Dictionary

definition of the word "hedge" is "to surround for defense; to fortify." The Hebrew definition of the word hedge is "(Gadar) to wall in, enclose, fence up." If you recall, there is another mention of a hedge in the book of Job where Satan observed God's hedge of protection around Job, his family, and his belongings.

> And the LORD said unto Satan, Hast thou considered my servant Job, that there is none like him in the earth, a perfect and an upright man, one that feareth God, and escheweth [avoids] evil? Then Satan answered the LORD, and said, Doth Job fear God for nought? Hast not thou made an hedge about him, and about his house, and about all that he hath on every side?
>
> Job 1:8–10

It is important to note that God's hedge of protection in this account was a direct result and benefit of Job's pure love for God, his obedience to God, his fear of God, and his commitment to avoid all manner of temptation and sin in his life. The hedge of protection that God places around our lives is simply one of the benefits of an obedient and intimate love relationship with Him. However, problems begin when we break our focus on God and begin to entertain tempting spirits. This is what Solomon meant in the Ecclesiastes 10:8 scripture, "whoso breaketh an hedge." The fact is, a broken hedge results in sin's deadly entrance into our lives. As we also read in the Ecclesiastes 10:8 scripture, once we let our hedge of protection or guard down, then a serpent will come in and bite us, hence envenomization or the entrance of sin occurs. Once we have allowed sin into our system, whether we like it or not, it *is* going to run its painful course, damaging anything and everything that it comes in contact with. Never forget, no matter how carefree or void of consequence Satan may present or package sin, its results are *never* without damaging and eventual deadly circumstances.

Just as a snakebite victim must suffer through the excruciating effects of a venomous bite, we too must suffer through the devastating effects of sin once we have allowed it to enter our lives. There is only one way to counteract the deadly effects of hematoxic or neurotoxic venom once it has entered the body: the immediate administration of an antivenom. The only way we can overcome the deadly effects of sin in our lives is to immediately administer what I like to call the "anti-sin'om" of confession and true repentance. Jesus says, "If we confess our sins, he is faithful and just to forgive us our sins, and to cleanse us from all unrighteousness" (1 John 1:9). However, the longer one waits to counteract the effects of sin the more devastating the final outcome will be. In order to avoid the painful effects of sin in our lives, we must follow Job's example of complete avoidance of all temptation. "Wherefore come out from among them, and be ye separate, saith the Lord, and touch not the unclean thing; and I will receive you, And will be a Father unto you, and ye shall be my sons and daughters, saith the Lord Almighty" (2 Corinthians 6:17–18). My earlier advice applies even more here. "When confronted by temptation, turn immediately and run for your life!"

As I began researching the effects of hematoxins and neurotoxins on the human body, I could not help but notice how closely they paralleled the definition of a word that I was researching for an earlier study on ignorance. The word that I am referring to is "stupid"! The Webster's Dictionary defines "stupid" as "very dull; insensible; senseless; wanting in understanding; heavy; sluggish; without the exercise of reason or judgment; numbness, etc." Hence the title of this message! *Sin Makes Ya Stewpit.* When we yield to temptation and thereby invite sin into our lives, like Adam and Eve, we simply exchange access to God himself, His wisdom, knowledge, peace, provision, understanding, discernment, and so much more for a fleeting moment of carnal pleasure. If you ask me, I'd say, "That's stupid!" Like a fire that rages through a beautiful forest destroying everything in its path, sin leaves the heart, mind, and soul charred and lifeless. Webster's defines "sin" as "the voluntary departure of a moral agent from a known rule of rectitude or duty, prescribed by God; any voluntary transgression of the divine law, or violation of a divine command; a wicked act; iniquity." I however like to define sin for what it really is: "anything that separates us from our wonderful Heavenly Father."

The solution to the sin problem in our lives is really very simple. If we don't want to suffer the traumatic effects of a snake's deadly bite, don't touch 'em! Likewise, if we don't want to suffer the pains of separation from God or the deadly effects of sin, i.e. stupidity, then don't touch it either! When tempting spirits come knocking on the door of your hedge (and they will), simply don't answer it. James instructs us, "Submit yourselves therefore to God. Resist the devil, and he will flee from you. Draw nigh to God, and he will draw nigh to you" (James 4:7–8). Pursue God with all of your heart, stay in His Word, and meditate on it day and night! "Thy word have I hid in mine heart, that I might not sin against thee" (Psalm 119:11).

If there has ever been a time to inspect the hedge around our lives for breakage, it is now! Fortify yourself with continual meditation on both God and His Word. Stay in continual communication with Him! "Pray without ceasing" (1 Thessalonians 5:17). Don't look on anything unclean. Keep company with people that love the Lord with all of their hearts. "He that walketh with wise men shall be wise: but a companion of fools shall be destroyed" (Proverbs 13:20). If there is a particular person or group of people that is weakening your relationship with God, walk away now! "Wherefore come out from among them, and be ye separate, saith the Lord, and touch not the unclean thing; and I will receive you, And will be a Father unto you, and ye shall be my sons and daughters, saith the Lord Almighty" (2 Corinthians 6:17–18). And when Satan comes around trying to make you regret putting your old ways and friends behind you (and he will), just remember what Jesus promised you: "Verily I say unto you, There is no man that hath left house, or parents, or brethren, or wife, or children, for the kingdom of God's sake, Who shall not receive manifold more in this present time, and in the world to come life everlasting" (Luke 18:29–30). Think about it for a moment, everything you've got for everything God's got! I've managed several multi-million dollar grossing companies over the past twenty years, and I can tell you for a fact that no better deal has ever been brokered!

Our Lord's triumphal return is much closer than we think! If we want to be included in His divine plan for these last days, we cannot be burdened down by the weight of sin. We must be free to receive and carry out our orders from the General of the soon-coming host of heaven. We must totally commit ourselves to staying pure in His sight at any cost. Repent of any sin that you may have allowed into your life, the ones you know of as well as the ones of which you are not even aware. This is key to our being effective at reaching those who don't know Jesus. The time to reach those around us with the life-giving and life-saving message of Jesus Christ is now! "The fruit of the righteous is a tree of life; and he that winneth souls is wise" (Proverbs 11:30). I encourage you to step out boldly and present the Gospel to your friends, classmates, coworkers, and fellow church members. Bind in the name of Jesus Christ the intimidating spirits that will try to hinder you, and go for it! The reality is that you just might be the last opportunity they have to accept Jesus! Don't let them down! "And they overcame him [Satan] by the blood of the Lamb, and by the word of their testimony; and they loved not their lives unto the death" (Revelation 12:11).

The Crisis of Eroding Integrity

Are you aware that there was actually a time in our nation's history when a person's word was their bond? When an agreement was made, the parties involved would simply shake hands, and it was done. I remember very clearly when I was around the age of seven watching my great grandfather negotiate a price to do some construction work for a man. They went back and forth for a while and finally came to an agreement. Then they shook hands, and off we went. There was no need for lengthy and confusing contracts to keep the transaction and those involved honest. People simply lived their lives based on the integrity of the honor system. They took to heart and practiced this command, "But let your communication be, Yea, yea; Nay, nay: for whatsoever is more than these cometh of evil" (Matthew 5:37).

However, integrity is much more than simply saying what you mean and meaning what you say. According to Webster's Dictionary, "integrity" is, the entire, unimpaired state of anything, particularly of mind; moral soundness or purity; incorruptness; uprightness; honesty. Integrity comprises the whole moral character, but has a special reference to uprightness in mutual dealings, transfers of property, and agencies for others.

As good as this definition may be, it still falls short of the way God defines integrity. Integrity in God's eyes is the character of the Lord Jesus Christ! Jesus died for us on the cross to pay the penalty for our sins and to provide the way for us to live godly lives. "For he hath made him to be sin for us, who knew no sin; that we might be made the righteousness of God in him" (2 Corinthians 5:21).

Integrity is so much more than attending church regularly or doing good deeds. The condition of the heart determines whether or not a person is walking in integrity. "A good man out of the good treasure of the heart bringeth forth good things" (Matthew 12:35). This good treasure includes honesty in business dealings, personal affairs, and family matters. People who walk in integrity always leave legacies that live on long after they are gone. "The just man walketh in his integrity: his children are blessed after him" (Proverbs 20:7).

Since 1979, I have been blessed by God by having a close relationship with a pastor who meets the Biblical standard of a true shepherd. I have also had the privilege of spending time with many other wonderfully-anointed Christian leaders. These folks are godly men and women of faith who have modeled for me and so many others just what it means to walk out a life of integrity in every situation. They are passionate about truth; they love others unconditionally; and they are selfless and have "in deed" given their whole lives for the purpose of seeing God's perfect will and plan fulfilled in everything they do. When they tell you that they are going to do something, you can take it to the bank! They are truly priceless gifts from our wonderful God to us all and are rightfully due the utmost honor and respect! "And he gave some, apostles; and some, prophets; and some, evangelists; and some, pastors and teachers; For the perfecting of the saints, for the work of the ministry, for the edifying of the body of Christ" (Ephesians 4:11–12). "Most men will proclaim every one his own goodness: but a faithful man who can find?" (Proverbs 20:6). True leaders in the Church exemplify the character of the Lord Jesus Christ. On the other hand, there are many in the Church who have not behaved honorably, as the all too frequent stories in the news demonstrate: pastors who rob their churches in more ways than one; "Christian" businessmen who manipulate their clients and cheat their employees; and so on. People hear these stories and wag their fingers at the Church, saying, "Christians are all just a bunch of hypocrites." This is so often the reason why people refuse to believe the message of the Gospel, not realizing that the name of Christ is being slandered by being falsely associated with people who are not walking in integrity.

Having at best very little regard for truth, these people have left a deadly trail of broken promises behind them. Rather than being wonderful, life-giving examples of Christlikeness, they are instead examples of how Jesus says not to be. As a result of this lack of integrity, many have and are suffering in many different ways. No matter how you cut it, these broken commitments have caused disillusionment and rejection in the lives of the people to whom the promises were made. Make no mistake about it, this is a serious spiritual matter. Jesus Himself issues a very stern warning in the scriptures when He says,

> And whoso shall receive one such little child in my name receiveth me. But whoso shall offend one of these little ones which believe in me, it were better for him that a millstone were hanged about his neck, and that he were drowned in the depth of the sea. Woe unto the world because of offences! for it must needs be that offences come; but woe to that man by whom the offence cometh!
>
> Matthew 18:5–7

When someone repeatedly breaks their word, they frequently cause others to doubt the Word of God also, thereby causing others to stumble (the literal meaning of the Greek word translated "offend").

Whether we are in leadership or not, we have to get serious about better protecting the hearts of anyone God places in our lives. The way we do this is by simply keeping our word to them. Webster's Dictionary defines "lying" as "to make a statement one knows is false; to bring, put, accomplish, etc. by lying—a false statement made with the intent to deceive." How is that different from telling someone you are going to do something and then not doing it? Good intentions will never make up for failure to follow through. When we tell God or anyone else that we are going to do something but then turn around and don't fulfill that commitment, it not only inflicts pain on them, but in turn it also reveals the lack of integrity operating in our own lives. To the persons who heard your commitment and saw your subsequent failure to honor it, it does not matter what your intentions were. The result is the same as if you had deliberately misled them, resulting in the offense of one or more of *His* little ones. And that, in and of itself, will erode your reputation in the Church and community almost as quickly as practicing any other sinful act will. Be informed, a person who says one thing and does another is, in fact, a detriment to God, to everything that He is trying to do, and to everyone else around them! "When thou vowest a vow unto God, defer not to pay it; for he hath no pleasure in fools: pay that which thou hast vowed. Better is it that thou shouldest not vow, than that thou shouldest vow and not pay" (Ecclesiastes 5:4–5). Did you notice that the writer actually refers to a person who does not keep his word to God as a fool?

Jesus takes it a step further, clarifying and emphasizing the importance of, in this case, breaking a vow or promise to anyone. "Verily I say unto you, Inasmuch as ye have done it unto one of the least of these my brethren, ye have done it unto me" (Matthew 25:40). When we keep our word to someone, it is the same as keeping our word to Jesus. Conversely, breaking our word with someone is the same as breaking our word with God!

Are you aware of just how many precious Christians have been temporarily and even permanently damaged both emotionally and spiritually because a lukewarm leader repeatedly told them one thing and did another? "A double minded man is unstable in all his ways" (James 1:8). I am not just talking about a professional hireling that leads the proverbial cold little church on the backside of a mountain somewhere. This also includes any one of us who fails to maintain integrity in every aspect of our lives. "A false balance is abomination to the LORD: but a just weight is his delight" (Proverbs 11:1).

I have personally met and worked to help restore hundreds of these hurting people over my own twenty-five plus years in ministry. This kind of thing is devastating and should never take place, or even be so much as mentioned in the life of the Church! Remember what Jesus said, "But whoso shall offend one of these little ones which believe in me, it were better for him that a millstone were hanged about his neck, and that he were drowned in the depth of the sea!" (Matthew 18:6).

If you are leading a group of God's people in any capacity and have fallen into the trap of thinking that you are exempt from fulfilling your obligations to them because of your own perceived loftiness of the position you hold, you are not only deceived, but you are also setting yourself up for a terrible fall. "Pride goeth before destruction, and an haughty spirit before a fall" (Proverbs 16:18). Jesus said,

> The kings of the Gentiles exercise lordship over them; and they that exercise authority upon them are called benefactors. But ye shall not be so: but he that is greatest among you, let him be as the younger; and he that is chief, as he that doth serve. For whether is greater, he that sitteth at meat, or he that serveth? is not he that sitteth at meat? but I am among you as he that serveth.
>
> Luke 22:25–27

It all boils down to this: If you are going to tell someone that you will do something, you had better think it through very carefully before you make the commitment! "For which of you, intending to build a tower, sitteth not down first, and counteth the cost, whether he have sufficient to finish it?" (Luke 14:28). A broken vow is an offense that carries a very stiff sentence in the eyes of God! Do not be deceived, this can be something as simple as our telling someone that we are going to pray for them, but we don't, or telling someone that we will call or stop by, and we don't. Listen to what Jesus warns us of concerning these vows made in passing: "But I say unto you, That every idle word that men shall speak, they shall give account thereof in the day of judgment.

For by thy words thou shalt be justified, and by thy words thou shalt be condemned" (Matthew 12:36–37).

There is no way around it, whenever a person says one thing and does another, it is lying and will be judged as such! These are some of the "little foxes" that are stealing the fruit from our vines (Song of Solomon 2:15)! Integrity must be the hallmark of our lives if we are going to be effective at verbally communicating and modeling the word of God to people! There is no way around it! We must make sure our yea means yea and our nay means nay. We must speak the Truth and live the Truth! We must say what we mean and mean what we say. Don't say you're going to do something and then not follow through. Jesus wouldn't!

Too Quick to Compromise

Anyone who is in pursuit of an intimate relationship with God will be presented at times with opportunities to compromise that relationship. Much like Esau sold his entire birthright to his brother Jacob for a piece of bread, a bowl of beans, and something to drink, we have all had times in our lives when we have been enticed away from both God and our own inheritance in Him to pursue idols or little "g" gods. You know who and what they are: relationships with the wrong people; the selfish pursuit of prominence in the eyes of those around us; escapisms like drugs, shopping, pornography, TV, alcohol, etc. No matter how long we have been a Christian, we can always count on spirits of temptation doing anything and everything they can to try to lure us away from God and into the jaws of compromising situations whose "reward" is always death or separation from God. This is, after all, the true definition of death itself! "But every man is tempted, when he is drawn away of his own lust, and enticed. Then when lust hath conceived, it bringeth forth sin: and sin, when it is finished, bringeth forth death" (James 1:14-15).

As Christians, it is of the utmost importance that we understand what sin really is. When most people hear the word "sin" mentioned, their first thought or impression is usually substance abuse, illicit sex, murder, stealing, and the like. It really goes so much deeper than that! These offenses are referred to as sins because they drive a wedge between us and God. That is what sin really is, anything that separates us from our Heavenly Father! It really is that simple! If we truly cherish God and want to grow in our relationship with Him, we must learn that temptation is Satan's primary weapon in the war to lure us away from God. Did you know that one of the very first things that a new recruit in the Armed Forces is taught is how to recognize both his enemy and their tactics? The reason they do this is so that our troops in the field will have an advantage over their adversaries. This information not only gives our soldiers an edge in defending themselves, but it also gives them a strategic advantage when preparing to launch an offensive. Without this crucial information, our soldiers in harm's way will most likely be defeated before they even hit the battlefield. It works the same way with those of us who are in God's army. If we are going to be victorious in defeating Satan's attempts at separating us from God, then we must first equip ourselves with a "heart knowledge" of God's Word, and then we must familiarize ourselves with what Satan has in his divisive arsenal. "My people are destroyed for lack of knowledge" (Hosea 4:6). Please don't take that statement out of context! The truth is, if we spend more time chasing demons around than we spend pursuing and spending time with God, we will eventually find ourselves in a "world of hurt"! On the other hand, if we passionately pursue God, learn His Word, and obey His Word, everything else will take care of itself! If we do not, we will be easy prey when tempting spirits come a knockin'! "But seek ye first the kingdom of God, and his righteousness; and all these things shall be added unto you" (Matthew 6:33).

Here is how Webster's Dictionary defines "tempt," "1) to entice or induce, as to something immoral, 2) to be inviting to; attract, 3) to provoke or risk provoking, 4) to incline strongly." Tempting spirits work to manipulate each one of us into compromising situations. Just like certain species of snakes travel in pairs, wherever temptation is present, the opportunity to compromise our relationship with God will always be somewhere close by. "But every man is tempted, when he is drawn away of his own lust, and enticed. Then when lust hath conceived, it bringeth forth sin: and sin, when it is finished, bringeth forth death" (James 1:14–15). "Submit yourselves therefore to God. Resist the devil, and he will flee from you" (James 4:7). "Blessed is the man that endureth temptation: for when he is tried, he shall receive the crown of life, which the Lord hath promised to them that love him" (James 1:12). Simply put, temptation is what Satan uses to present us with opportunities for compromise.

Now that we have laid some groundwork, let's take a look at the main topic in the title of our message, the word "compromise." Webster's defines "compromise" as "1) a settlement in which each side makes concessions, 2) something midway, 3) to adjust by compromise, 4) to lay open to suspicion, disrepute, etc." The word "disrepute" is defined as "bad reputation; disgrace." Noah Webster's 1828 edition defines "compromise" as "to put to hazard." However, my personal definition of compromise is, "the act of trading one's relationship with God for anything else."

There are many potentially dangerous distractions in the world today. With lawlessness increasing in the earth at a staggering rate, we are seeing, as a result, compromise becoming a regular way of life for many who claim to be Christians; and frankly, the present condition of the Church confirms it. Things that were unheard of in the Church just two decades ago are now being practiced without remorse. While Timothy was overseeing the Church in Ephesus, Paul wrote warning him that this would happen. "Now the Spirit speaketh expressly, that in the latter times some shall depart from the faith, giving heed to seducing spirits, and doctrines of devils; Speaking lies in hypocrisy; having their conscience seared with a hot iron" (1 Timothy 4:1–2). When we compromise our relationship with God in any way, what we are doing is turning our backs on Him. We are actually saying that something or someone else is more important to us than He is. Not only does this hurt His heart deeply, but it also says to those who have heard you profess to be a Christian that God must not really be who you or His Word says He is.

"Howbeit, because by this deed thou hast given great occasion to the enemies of the Lord to blaspheme, the child also that is born unto thee shall surely die"(2 Samuel 12:14). I would like to share with you one such situation that I experienced and will follow it up with a brief teaching on a related subject that for years has been a major stronghold in the lives of thousands of people in the Church.

One evening I was invited to dinner by the pastor of a local church who had heard a few of my songs at some point and said that he would like to get to know me. I had met this person on several occasions in passing and had heard through some friends that he was doing a good work in the community. Based on that information, I accepted his offer. Once we had arrived at the restaurant, we were seated for what I thought was going to be a very nice evening. We were about halfway through the meal when he flagged our waiter back to the table. Much to my astonishment, he then leaned back in his chair, acquired a rather sheepish-looking grin, and proceeded to order a pitcher of beer. Knowing what I had heard about this person, I have to say that I was stunned. I found myself headlong in the presence of yet another professing Christian who was "too quick to compromise!"

I fought to maintain my composure as best I could and continued eating my meal. Within seconds righteous indignation began welling up in me to the point that my self-control was being tested. As my momma would have said, "I felt like I was gonna pop if I didn't say something." I did the best I could to remain cool while all the time listening for the Lord's approval to confront him. "Brethren, if a man be overtaken in a fault, ye which are spiritual, restore such an one in the spirit of meekness; considering thyself, lest thou also be tempted" (Galatians 6:1).

It was not until two days later that I felt a release in my spirit to talk with him about it. I then called him and asked if he would join me for lunch. As soon as the Holy Spirit gave me the nod, I gently asked him this question. "As a Christian, and especially as a self-professed minister of the Gospel, why do you feel that it is all right for you to drink alcohol?" As soon as those words left my mouth, I found myself on the receiving end of a bitter attack. Much like spraying water on a wasps' nest I very quickly realized that I had touched an area of compromise in this fellow's life that he was not really interested in turning loose of any time soon. Almost without stopping to breathe, he began hurling scriptures at me attempting to justify his actions. I sat there quietly and let him state his case. When he had finished, with all of the love I could muster, I simply asked if he would be open to hearing my point of view concerning Christians and alcohol use. "A soft answer turneth away wrath: but grievous words stir up anger" (Proverbs 15:1).

Taking the defensive posture of crossing his arms, tightening his brow, and setting his jaw, he slid back in his seat obviously hunkering down for what he thought was going to be a major offensive. I then referenced several scriptures and asked him to share with me how he felt they could in any way be used to justify his or any other Christian's consumption of alcohol. After a brief period of time, it became increasingly clear that he could not Biblically justify Christians drinking alcoholic beverages. Apparently frustrated, he then pulled out what I believe he thought would settle the matter—he said, "Well, Jesus drank wine." I knew at that very moment that I had been divinely presented with a wonderful opportunity to help him understand what has become a major point of deception, confusion, and compromise for thousands of people who claim to be born-again Christians.

This is what I shared with him. During the time when Jesus physically walked the earth, they had no way of purifying their drinking water. Because of this, they relied heavily on fruit juice as their primary means of safe and nourishing hydration. They also had no way of refrigerating or preserving juices that had been derived from their fruit harvest. When they would extract the fresh juice from the fruit, they would store it in small leather sacks called wine skins. This *fresh* juice was referred to as "wine." This is where many people in the Church today have been and are being terribly deceived. In Christ's day, the best wine was always the freshest fruit juice. For example, the first miracle that Jesus performed was actually turning water into wine or fresh fruit juice. Here is how John recorded the event:

And the third day there was a marriage in Cana of Galilee; and the mother of Jesus was there: And both Jesus was called, and his disciples, to the marriage. And when they wanted wine, the mother of Jesus saith unto him, They have no wine. Jesus saith unto her, Woman, what have I to do with thee? mine hour is not yet come. [This statement is a whole other story.] His mother saith unto the servants, Whatsoever he saith unto you, do it. And there were set there six waterpots of stone, after the manner of the purifying of the Jews, containing two or three firkins apiece. [A firkin was about nine gallons.] Jesus saith unto them, Fill the waterpots with water. And they filled them up to the brim. [All told there were about 162 gallons.] And he saith unto them, Draw out now, and bear unto the governor of the feast. And they bare it. [They poured him a drink and gave it to him.] When the ruler of the feast had tasted the water that was made wine, and knew not whence it was: (but the servants which drew the water knew) the governor of the feast called the bridegroom, And saith unto him, Every man at the beginning doth set forth good wine; and when men have well drunk, then that which is worse: but thou hast kept the good wine until now.

John 2:1–10

In other words, the governor of the feast was totally amazed at the fact that the juice was so fresh! It was as if it had just been picked and squeezed all within that same hour, when—in a matter of speaking—it had been! The society back then was for the most part very moral and would never even think of bringing strong drink or "the old stuff" to such a sacred event. That would have been a devastating insult to all in attendance! Believe it or not, anyone who drank "old wine" or fermented drink was viewed by society much like we view someone who eats out of a dumpster.

On the other hand, it is not like that today! In our present culture, things have become so turned around that wine is the name given to fruit juice that has gone bad through the process of fermentation. It is this fermentation process that produces the alcohol in it. It is of the utmost importance that we realize that there were varying stages of fermentation. In other words, each week that the wine sat in the bottles it would ferment more and more. Due to the lack of refrigeration, the fermentation process literally began taking place during the first week that the juice was stored in the wine skins. The time that it took to ferment was in great part determined by the temperature at which it was stored. Because the fruit harvest was done in the warmer part of the season, the wine skins would have naturally been stored in warm conditions. The longer the juice sat in warm climates, the stronger or more fermented it became. That is why the word "wine" was a blanket term used to describe the juice at each of its various stages of fermentation. For instance, wine that was three weeks old would have developed a little bite to it; wine that was seven weeks old would have a bigger bite; and so on. Once it had come to full age, however, it was not to be consumed. When it reached that point, it was no longer referred to as wine, but was referred to as strong or fermented drink, and was to be thrown out! "Look not thou upon the wine when it is red, when it giveth his colour in the cup, when it moveth itself aright. At the last [meaning when it has fermented] it biteth like a serpent, and stingeth like an adder"(Proverbs 23:31–32). That scripture was a warning to stay away from the juice once it had sat around too long and had fermented or "gone bad."

Unless you are on your deathbed, the Bible does not, never has, and never will condone the consumption of strong or fermented drink for the purpose of becoming, even in the slightest bit, mentally impaired! As a matter of fact, the only place in the scriptures where the consumption of strong or fermented drink was justifiably permitted at all was in Proverbs 31:6 where King Lemuel had recited a prophecy that his mother taught him. He said, "Give strong drink unto him that is ready to perish, and wine unto those that be of heavy hearts." The heavyhearted were never permitted to drink strong or fermented drink; only the dying were! And that was simply for the purpose of relieving them of any pain they might suffer in the final days before they expired. Strong or fermented drink was *never* intended to be used for any other reason! Can you see how Satan has been able to take advantage of the Church's lack of knowledge concerning the consumption of alcoholic beverages? By keeping this a "gray" issue as he has, he has been able to corral untold millions of churchgoers into a lukewarm life of compromise, hence destroying any ability they might have to conduct a pure and close personal relationship with God. "My people are destroyed for lack of knowledge: because thou hast rejected knowledge, I will also reject thee, that thou shalt be no priest to me: seeing thou hast forgotten the law of thy God, I will also forget thy children" (Hosea 4:6).

It is time to wake up and realize that this is simply another ploy of our enemy to separate God's people from God and all of the wonderful things that He has for them. "Wine is a mocker, strong drink is raging: and whosoever is deceived thereby is not wise" (Proverbs 20:1). Compromise in any form will always serve to ultimately cost us in our relationship with God! Whether it is alcohol, the abuse of street or prescription drugs, food, television, or anything else, Satan is constantly working to get his foot in the door of our lives to ultimately impair our ability to hear the voice of our loving Heavenly Father.

See then that ye walk circumspectly, not as fools, but as wise, Redeeming the time, because the days are evil. Wherefore be ye not unwise, but understanding what the will of the Lord is. And be not drunk with wine, wherein is excess; but be filled with the Spirit; Speaking to yourselves in psalms and hymns and spiritual songs, singing and making melody in your heart to the Lord; Giving thanks always for all things unto God and the Father in the name of our Lord

Jesus Christ; Submitting yourselves one to another in
the fear of God.

Ephesians 5:15–21

We must come to the place in our hearts where
we know without a shadow of a doubt that, "There is
nobody or nothing worth our relationship with Jesus!"

Please...Stop Stinkin'

Are you aware that everything we do or say in life, like rising smoke from a campfire, goes up before the throne of Almighty God as a sweet fragrance or as a putrid stench? Paul, commending the saints in Philippi for their obedience to the things of God, wrote:

> For even in Thessalonica ye sent once and again unto my necessity. Not because I desire a gift: but I desire fruit that may abound to your account. But I have all, and abound: I am full, having received of Epaphroditus the things which were sent from you, an odour of a sweet smell, a sacrifice acceptable, well-pleasing to God.
>
> Philippians 4:16–18

Paul made reference again to a "sweet smell" when he was encouraging the Ephesians to love others in the same way that Jesus does. He said, "And walk in love, as Christ also hath loved us, and hath given himself for us an offering and a sacrifice to God for a sweetsmelling savour" (Ephesians 5:2). Can this be said of you?

Does the smoke from your life that continuously rises up before the throne of Almighty God put a smile on His face or does it turn His stomach? If the latter is the case, I have a message for you straight from God Himself, "Please . . . stop stinkin'!"

Sadly enough, each of us at some point in our lives has been exposed to someone that, how shall I say this, just outright stunk! Whether in school, at work, or somewhere else, most of us can recall at some point suffering the discomforts of being subjected to the "hygienically challenged." The fact is, if we do not daily apply the time and effort needed to maintain physical cleanliness in our lives, then we will inevitably offend the vast majority of those that we come in contact with, especially those who practice good personal hygiene themselves. The same can be said of our spiritual lives. Paul, emphasizing the utter importance of purity in his instruction of the men of Ephesus on how they should treat their wives, said,

> Husbands, love your wives, even as Christ also loved the church, and gave himself for it; that he might sanctify and cleanse it with the washing of water by the word, that he might present it to himself a glorious church, not having spot, or wrinkle, or any such thing; but that it should be holy and without blemish.
>
> Ephesians 5:25–27

As I read this scripture, I was drawn to the word "blemish," especially since it is something that we are not to be if our lives are to give off a "sweet smell." I grabbed my trusty old dictionary and started digging. As I read through the various descriptions of the word "blemished," I discovered something rather interesting. As one of its definitions I found the word "soiled." I then looked up the word "soiled" and found as one of its definitions the word "sully." Having never heard the word "sully" used in any conversation that I have ever been a part of, I almost ignored it. But curious about its meaning, I went ahead and looked it up as well. I was glad that I did! I found that the very first definition of "sully" was "to soil; to dirt; to spot; to tarnish. Sullied yet with sacrilegious smoke." I was immediately drawn to the term "sacrilegious smoke," especially since it ties so well into the context of this topic.

What is "sacrilegious smoke"? Since we all pretty much know what smoke is, I once again referred to the pages of my dictionary to see what it had to say about the word "sacrilegious." It simply said, "The violation of sacred things." Keeping in context with the first paragraph of our letter, it would stand to reason that sacrilegious smoke would, in fact, be something that smells terribly offensive to God. Now, if the violation of sacred things (meaning disobedience to "God's Word") is displeasing to Him, then what would it take to please God? The answer is simple—obedience to His Word and His Word alone! "If ye be willing and obedient, ye shall eat the good of the land: but if ye refuse and rebel, ye shall be devoured with the sword: for the mouth of the Lord hath spoken it" (Isaiah 1:19–20). Throughout all of scripture, willing obedience to "God's Word" has been the key to bringing joy to His heart!

In keeping with the tradition of this study thus far, let's take a look at the word "obedience." In that same dictionary, "obedience" is defined as "submissive to authority; yielding compliance with commands, orders or injunctions; performing what is required, or abstaining from what is forbidden." Question: how can we be submissive to authority if we do not invest the time and effort needed to familiarize ourselves with the will of the one in authority? Paul teaches us, "Servants, obey in all things your masters according to the flesh; not with eyeservice, as menpleasers; but in singleness of heart, fearing God" (Colossians 3:22). How can we truly obey a master with whom we are not familiar? It is simply not possible if we do not have an intimate knowledge of both our Master and His requirements or laws! The same is true regarding our relationship with Jesus! John teaches us, "He that saith, I know him, and keepeth not his commandments, is a liar, and the truth is not in him" (1 John 2:4). It is not enough to say we love Jesus, we must show our love by keeping His commands. Jesus said, "He that hath my commandments, and keepeth them, he it is that loveth me: and he that loveth me shall be loved of my Father, and I will love him, and will manifest myself to him" (John 14:21).

In order to be pleasing to God, we must love Him with our whole heart and fall passionately in love with His Word. We must regularly study the scriptures and put them into practice in our everyday lives! This must be our way of life! James wrote,

> But be ye doers of the word, and not hearers only, deceiving your own selves. For if any be a hearer of the word, and not a doer, he is like unto a man beholding his natural face in a glass: For he beholdeth himself, and goeth his way, and straightway forgetteth what manner of man he was. But whoso looketh into the perfect law of liberty, and continueth therein, he being not a forgetful hearer, but a doer of the work, this man shall be blessed in his deed.
>
> James 1:22–25

You see, doers of the Word will be pleasing to God because their lives will, by nature, give off smoke that rises up before His throne as a sweet fragrance. On the other hand, being a hearer of God's Word and not a doer of it will generate from one's life the "sacrilegious smoke" or putrid odor that was mentioned a moment ago. Paul said, "For not the hearers of the law are just before God, but the doers of the law shall be justified" (Romans 2:13). Disobedience to God's Word fuels the fire that produces sacrilegious smoke or an offensive odor from our lives.

Now, let's take this a step further up and further in! What is the Word of God? Whenever I ask or have asked this question in various group settings, except for a few, the response is always the same. They raise their Bibles in the air and shout, "This is God's Word!"

However, as true as that is, it still falls short of God's original purpose for giving us the scriptures. God's written Word or the Bible was never intended to be an end in and of itself, but to be a means to an end! That end is our intimate relationship with Him. Paul said in his letter to the Romans, "So then faith cometh by hearing, and hearing by the word of God" (Romans 10:17).

Just as Paul told his disciples, "Be ye followers of me, even as I also am of Christ" (1 Corinthians 11:1), we are to follow this same example where the scriptures are concerned.

> This book of the law shall not depart out of thy mouth; but thou shalt meditate therein day and night, that thou mayest observe to do according to all that is written therein: for then thou shalt make thy way prosperous, and then thou shalt have good success.
>
> Joshua 1:8

In other words, as we are faithful to meditate on the written Word of God, the time will eventually come when we will enter the place where we will actually hear the Spoken Word or Voice of God. This is where the fullness of life really begins! It is really very simple; reading the written Word of God prepares us to recognize and hear the voice of God! This is what Jesus meant when he said, "It is written, 'Man shall not live by bread alone, but by every word that proceedeth out of the mouth of God'" (Matthew 4:4). The primary reason that much of the Church is in the impotent condition that it is in today is because so few of her members have been taught that the written Word of God is simply the doorway into our being able to recognize and hear the spoken Word, or the voice of God Himself. Our obtaining the ability to both hear and obey God's voice is what enables us to possess the most valuable prize of all, a close and intimate relationship with the true and living God!

Do you see why it is so important that we learn and obey the written Word of God? It lays the groundwork for our being able to hear God when He speaks to us. It is only by His spoken Word or voice that we can receive His anointing and can be led into all good things. "Thy word is a lamp unto my feet, and a light unto my path" (Psalm 119:105). A life lived solely by the written Word of God will by nature be beneficial to anyone who lives by it. But if we want the abundant life that Jesus came to provide, we must diligently seek Him with our whole heart, listen for, and obey His every word! "The thief cometh not, but for to steal, and to kill, and to destroy: I am come that they might have life, and that they might have it more abundantly" (John 10:10). We must know His voice! Jesus said, "My sheep hear my voice, and I know them, and they follow me: and I give unto them eternal life; and they shall never perish, neither shall any man pluck them out of my hand" (John 10:27–28). Those who hear and obey the voice of God will always send up a sweet-smelling savor that will bring pleasure to the heart of our wonderful King!

I would like to point out that the power that is

contained in God's voice is the most "wonder-filled" and awesome power, period! There are no words that can even begin to adequately describe it. I believe that if you were to ask King David just how accurate his description of God's voice was in Psalm 29, he would probably tell you that he wrote it down in the best way he knew how. I'm also pretty sure that he would follow that statement up with, "Truthfully, trying to describe God or His voice with words simply cannot be done!" Keeping this in mind, read this attempt by David to describe the indescribable.

> The voice of the LORD is powerful; the voice of the Lord is full of majesty. The voice of the Lord breaketh the cedars; yea, the Lord breaketh the cedars of Lebanon. He maketh them also to skip like a calf; Lebanon and Sirion like a young unicorn. The voice of the Lord divideth the flames of fire. The voice of the Lord shaketh the wilderness; the Lord shaketh the wilderness of Kadesh. The voice of the Lord maketh the hinds to calve, and discovereth the forests: and in his temple doth every one speak of his glory.
>
> Psalm 29:4–9

And don't forget it was that same voice that spoke everything into existence. "You be sweet now, ya hear!"

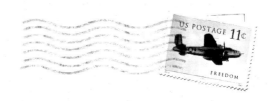

Let It Go

Early in the 1800s there was a ship loaded with gold headed to America from a foreign country. Several days into the journey, the ship and its crew found itself headlong in a ferocious storm. As the crew fought through the night to keep their beloved vessel afloat, it became increasingly obvious to all that they were rapidly losing to the monstrous waves and gale-force winds. Soon the hull of the ship began to break apart. After exhausting all options, the captain sent messengers who notified his crew to implement the most dreaded order that any captain has to give, "Abandon ship!"

While the majority of the crew were fighting to get the lifeboats overboard, several of the crew, who were not content with only getting away with their lives, went into the storage hold of the ship and proceeded to fill their pockets with gold. By the time they returned to the main deck, they found that the others had launched the lifeboats and had vanished into the darkness of night. With only a third of the ship still above water, they had to do something quickly. Looking at each other as if to say "We're rich!" they held on to the gold in their pockets and jumped into the sea. After just a few seconds, the weight of the gold and the frigid water began to exhaust the men. Rapidly each of them was confronted with a life or death decision: do I hold onto the gold and risk certain death, or do I turn it loose and greatly increase my chances of making it out of an already terrible situation? As you can well imagine, the guys who "let go" lived to tell the story, while the guys who held on greedily to the gold found their final resting place at the bottom of the ocean.

How many times in your walk with God have you found yourself in a similar situation—holding on to a relationship, your pride, an old way of thinking, things from the past, or anything else that has hindered you from moving further up and further in where your relationship with both God and His Word is concerned? If we are going to be able to move into the things that God has for us, we are going to have to become proficient at letting stuff go! Paul, knowing just how detrimental the past and the things that lie there can be to our future successes, teaches us, "Brethren, I count not myself to have apprehended: but this one thing I do, forgetting those things which are behind, and reaching forth unto those things which are before, I press toward the mark for the prize of the high calling of God in Christ Jesus" (Philippians 3:13–14). Understanding early on in my walk with our Lord that obtaining the ability to "let go" was so important to my pressing into the things of God, I chose to use this scripture as the hallmark declaration for this ministry. Hence the name, "Toward the Mark." So often we allow things into our lives that restrict our ability of "reaching forth unto those things which are before." Satan knows full well that if he can get us loaded up with enough stuff, he can essentially anchor us to the status quo, making any forward progress in our lives extremely difficult to achieve. A very wise man, who witnessed my spreading myself way too thin in the ministry, once pulled me aside and said something to me that would forever change my life. He simply told me that I needed to select my battles more wisely. The following is perhaps the best story that I have ever heard concerning someone who has mastered this.

In the winter of 1988, I was being interviewed by the host of a local radio station in the Washington, D.C. area in preparation for an upcoming concert that the band and I were scheduled to do. After we had been on the air for about ten minutes, the host announced to the listening audience that we were breaking for a few commercials. After we had broken away, the door to the studio opened, and in walked a local Messianic Jewish rabbi. Under his left arm he was carrying his briefcase, while in his right hand he was tossing a tennis ball up and down. Without warning he threw the tennis ball at the show's host. Seizing the moment as an opportunity to display his sharp athletic ability, the host immediately reached out and grabbed the tennis ball. As the host was starting to gloat a bit over his quick response to the pitch, the rabbi then looked him squarely in his eye and asked, "Why did you catch that ball?"

Looking rather puzzled, the host replied, "I don't know, I guess I've always been programmed to catch things when they were thrown at me."

At that, the rabbi asked him, "Do you know why Ronald Reagan was without a doubt one of the greatest world leaders that has ever lived?" The rabbi then continued, "The reason that Ronald Reagan was one of history's greatest leaders is because he learned how *not* to catch everything that was thrown at him!"

Until we finally come to the place where we know without a shadow of a doubt that there is nobody or nothing worth our relationship with God, we will continuously find ourselves drowning under the weightiness of the cares of this life. Jesus warns us,

> Heaven and earth shall pass away: but my words shall not pass away. And take heed to yourselves, lest at any time your hearts be overcharged with surfeiting [excess], and drunkenness, and cares of this life, and so that day come upon you unawares. For as a snare shall it come on all them that dwell on the face of the whole earth.
>
> Luke 21:33–35

Perhaps one of the best accounts of someone being presented with a fabulous opportunity to let go of something to pursue God is this story in Mark.

> And when he [Jesus] was gone forth into the way, there came one running, and kneeled to him, and asked

him, Good Master, what shall I do that I may inherit eternal life? And Jesus said unto him, Why callest thou me good? There is none good but one, that is, God. Thou knowest the commandments, Do not commit adultery, Do not kill, Do not steal, Do not bear false witness, Defraud not, Honour thy father and mother. And he answered and said unto him, Master, all these have I observed from my youth. Then Jesus beholding him, loved him, and said unto him, One thing thou lackest: go thy way, sell whatsoever thou hast, and give to the poor, and thou shalt have treasure in heaven: and come, take up the cross, and follow me. And he was sad at that saying, and went away grieved: for he had great possessions. And Jesus looked round about, and saith unto his disciples, How hardly shall they that have riches enter into the kingdom of God! And the disciples were astonished at his words. But Jesus answereth again, and saith unto them, Children, how hard is it for them that trust in riches to enter into the kingdom of God! It is easier for a camel to go through the eye of a needle, than for a rich man to enter into the kingdom of God. And they were astonished out of measure, saying among themselves, Who then can be saved? And Jesus looking upon them saith, With men it is impossible, but not with God: for with God all things are possible. Then Peter began to say unto him, Lo, we have left all, and have followed thee. And Jesus answered and said, Verily I say unto you, There is no man that hath left house, or brethren, or sisters, or father, or mother, or wife, or children, or lands, for my sake, and the gospel's, But he shall receive an hundredfold now in this time, houses, and brethren, and sisters, and mothers, and children, and lands, with persecutions; and in the world to come eternal life.

Mark 10:17–30

What a deal! We give God all that we have and He gives us what He has!

In the twenty-fifth verse of that chapter, Jesus made a statement that many have misunderstood for centuries. He said, "It is easier for a camel to go through the eye of a needle, than for a rich man to enter into the Kingdom of God." Even though many have thought so, He was not referring to the little hole in the end of a sewing needle. If that were the case, it would be impossible for anyone to enter the Kingdom of God. What Jesus was referring to however was a small opening in one of the walls that surrounded Jerusalem at the time. Though it was referred to as a gate, it was really very tiny by comparison to the other gates in the city's walls and was primarily used for access into the city after dark. This little hole in the wall, so to speak, was actually designed to protect Jerusalem from being attacked by armies in the night. Because this gate was so small, when anyone wanted to enter the city through it, they would have to leave their burdens or possessions outside the city, and make their camels or burros get down on their knees and literally crawl though it. When Jesus made reference to "a rich man" in this passage, He was not only referring to someone who had a lot of money. He was also referring to anyone that is weighed down with anything that hinders the pursuit of God. Remember, money is not the root of all evil; it is the love of it that traps us.

> But they that will be rich fall into temptation and a snare, and into many foolish and hurtful lusts, which drown men in destruction and perdition. For the love of money is the root of all evil: which while some coveted after, they have erred from the faith, and pierced themselves through with many sorrows.
>
> 1 Timothy 6:9–10

If we are going to pursue God, we must "let go" of anybody or anything we may have in our lives that would hinder our entrance into a close and personal relationship with Him!

As long as I have been serving both God and His people, perhaps one of the most heartbreaking things that I have witnessed has been Christians who have grown lukewarm in their walk with God due to the fact that they refuse to turn loose of a person, a group of people, or anything else in their lives that keeps them from moving into an intimate relationship with God. That is evidence of one of two things. Either they have a greater love for things that are contrary to the things of God, or they simply lack faith in God's ability to provide the abundant life that Christ came to give all who wholeheartedly trust in Him. "But without faith it is impossible to please him: for he that cometh to

God must believe that he is, and that he is a rewarder of them that diligently seek him" (Hebrews 11:6). If we are going to be pleasing to God, we are going to have to trust Him enough to take Him at His Word! "Wherefore lay apart all filthiness and superfluity of naughtiness, and receive with meekness the engrafted word, which is able to save your souls. But be ye doers of the word, and not hearers only, deceiving your own selves" (James 1:21–22).

When I was a youth pastor, I witnessed hundreds of heartbreaking cases of high school and college-aged people who, instead of waiting for God's best where a mate was concerned, grew impatient and settled for or pursued relationships with either unbelievers or, at best, lukewarm believers. In the vast majority of these cases, I found that the unbelieving or lukewarm partner always affected the believing partner with ungodliness much more than the believer ever affected the unbeliever with the things of God. Even though the believing partner went into the relationship thinking that they were going to win the unbeliever to Christ, the opposite almost always proved true. I am not saying that it is not possible, or that it has not been done. I am saying that, if you are going to pursue as your mate someone who does not love and serve God with their whole heart, you had better know without a shadow of a doubt that it is God's will for you and that those over you in the Lord are in agreement and are monitoring what you are doing very closely!

This mode of dating, referred to in many Christian

circles as "missionary dating," is in reality a very dangerous practice. It is practiced by many unmarried people in the Church but with increasing frequency by older people, as a result of their focusing on the seemingly narrowed field of available possibilities, instead of seeking the Lord. No matter what age you may be, participation in this deadly game of chance can leave you bound in chains that are very costly to break, both emotionally and financially! The same thing goes for any other aspect of our lives—whether we are seeking a mate, a new job, a new Church home, or anything else. Never forget, whenever we take something to ourselves that is not in God's will or timing for our lives, what we are doing is calling a curse down on our own heads. What truly pleases our wonderful God and King is our trusting in Him, resting in Him, and waiting on Him to perform, in His time, what His Word promises.

No matter how we slice it, the effects of sin are terribly weighty! Like a ship's anchor tied around our waist, or someone three times our size pinning our shoulders to the floor, the results of sin will always cost us our freedom, and ultimately can and will cost us our lives. Whether the burden you may be carrying is self-inflicted or a result of someone else's actions, it really does not matter. What does matter is becoming proficient at "letting them go and moving on with your life!" The apostle John wrote,

> This then is the message which we have heard of him,
> and declare unto you, that God is light, and in him is

no darkness at all. If we say that we have fellowship with him, and walk in darkness, we lie, and do not the truth: But if we walk in the light, as he is in the light, we have fellowship one with another, and the blood of Jesus Christ his Son cleanseth us from all sin. If we say that we have no sin, we deceive ourselves, and the truth is not in us. If we confess our sins, he is faithful and just to forgive us our sins, and to cleanse us from all unrighteousness.

1 John 1:5–9

You might ask, "What if the thing that I am struggling with is not a direct result of my committing a sinful act? What do I do then?" It is of the utmost importance that we first understand what sin really is. Sin is not simply illicit sex, drug abuse, murder, stealing, and the like. These are merely means by which sin gains access into our lives. Sin is actually anything that separates us from God Himself. It's that simple! Whether the sin in your life is self-inflicted or a result of a generational curse, it does not matter. Sin is sin and Jesus stands more than ready to forgive and deliver us from them all! So, if you know that things are not right between you and God, if your communication with Him has been cut off, do not panic. Take a deep breath, relax, examine your heart, confess your sins, and walk away from practicing whatever it was that gave the sin access into your life. Ask Jesus to forgive you, and move on with him. Remember, falling in the water is not what causes you to drown, it is staying there that will eventually cost you your life! "If we confess our sins, he [Jesus] is faithful and just to forgive us our sins, and to cleanse us from all unrighteousness" (1 John 1:9). Paul says,

> For I am persuaded, that neither death, nor life, nor angels, nor principalities, nor powers, nor things present, nor things to come, nor height, nor depth, nor any other creature, shall be able to separate us from the love of God, which is in Christ Jesus our Lord.
>
> Romans 8:38–39

Praise God for His divine forgiveness!

I would like to share a great little story with you that is very applicable to this teaching. In certain parts of Africa, monkeys are captured and sold for a number of different uses. Some are sold for research; some are sold to animal brokers, who in turn sell them to zoos or pet stores; and some are even sold to various regions of the world as a culinary delicacy. Because monkeys are so difficult to catch, the trappers have an ingenious way of capturing the animals without injuring them. They have taken a lesson from their ancient tribal ancestors. They find a gourd, and cut a small hole in the side of it just big enough for a monkey's hand. They put a chunk of hard food inside the gourd, and then tie the gourd in a tree. Once the trappers have strategically placed the gourd where they want it, they hide in the bush and wait for the monkeys. When a monkey smells the food, he very cautiously approaches the gourd. He looks inside, sees the food, and reaches in to get it. Unbeknownst to him, the hole that was large enough for his hand is too small for a fistful of food. The trappers then run out of the bush making loud noises. When the monkey hears them coming, he becomes so startled and confused that he does not think to turn loose of the food. The trappers then climb the tree, cut down the gourd—with the monkey's hand still in it—and place them both safely into a cage. If the monkey had only "let go" of the food, he would be free instead of either being served up in some restaurant or bound in captivity for life! I beseech you desperately, if there is anybody or anything in your life that is separating you from God, "*Let it go!*"

Into the Secret Place

Did you know that there is actually a place you can go where your inadequacies will totally melt away, where your sorrows are turned into joy, and where you can find out what you were put on this earth to be and to do? This "wonder-filled" place is the presence of God. Psalm 16:11 says this about God's presence, "in thy presence is fulness of joy; at thy right hand there are pleasures forevermore." The following verse in Psalms gives us one of the most profound instructions in all of the Bible concerning the importance of pursuing and living in the presence of God. "He that dwelleth in the secret place of the most High shall abide under the shadow of the Almighty" (Psalm 91:1).

In order to better understand what this means, let's take a moment and break this scripture down. The first statement in the verse says, "He that dwelleth in the secret place of the most High." The word "dwelleth" or "dwell" means to make one's home or to live. In other words, he who makes the presence of God his home will reap and enjoy the benefits of the second part of this scripture that says, they "shall abide under the shadow of the Almighty." The word "abide" finds its root in the word "abode," meaning home or residence. If we live our lives in God's presence, we will then, and only then, enjoy the benefits that come with being in relationship with Him.

This is what is meant by "abiding under the shadow of the Almighty." Under the shadow of the Almighty is the place where God protects, heals, provides, teaches, frees, changes, and so much more. It is crucial at this point to note that our entrance into the secret place is a result of diligently seeking God with our whole heart: for the secret place is reserved for those who love Him and are thankful to Him for who He is more than for what He does or can do. We must abide or live in God! Jesus said,

Abide in me, and I in you. As the branch cannot bear fruit of itself, except it abide in the vine; no more can ye, except ye abide in me. I am the vine, ye are the branches: he that abideth in me, and I in him, the same bringeth forth much fruit: for without me ye can do nothing. If a man abide not in me, he is cast forth as a branch, and is withered; and men gather them, and cast them into the fire, and they are burned. If ye abide in me, and my words abide in you, ye shall ask what ye will, and it shall be done unto you. Herein is my Father glorified, that ye bear much fruit; so shall ye be my disciples.

John 15:4–8

Many people in our churches today practice periodic visitation rather than permanent residency So many seek after the miracles of God rather than God Himself, not realizing that everything God does is for the purpose of establishing *ongoing* relationships with each one of us!

Even though God's works are amazing, to say the least, they were never intended to distract us from Himself. On the contrary, the miracles that Jesus performed during His earthly ministry, as well as those He performs today, were and are for one reason alone: to focus our attention on God and on the fact that He desires a close, loving relationship with each one of us. When we allow ourselves to become more focused on His deeds than on God Himself, we have allowed ourselves to be separated or severed from our source of life, and we will wither and die as Jesus teaches us. Paul addressed that very thing when he said, They "worshipped and served the creature more than the creator" (Romans 1:25). This is in fact the birthplace of idol worship and dead religion. This is where style becomes preferred and sought after more than substance, where more attention and effort is placed on seeking signs and wonders or on doing things a particular group's way than on pursuing God Himself. Herein lies the root cause of the Church's declining effectiveness in our communities! Paul dealt with this same problem in Corinth. To the Corinthians he wrote,

And what agreement hath the temple of God with idols? for ye are the temple of the living God; as God hath said, I will dwell in them, and walk in them; and I will be their God, and they shall be my people. Wherefore come out from among them, and be ye separate, saith the Lord, and touch not the unclean thing; and I will receive you, And will be a Father unto you, and ye shall be my sons and daughters, saith the Lord Almighty.

2 Corinthians 6:16–18

We are to be separate from everything and everyone that would keep us from being separate unto God. Never forget, sin is anything that separates us from God! This includes miracles. God does not intend for miracles to distract us from Him.

Never before have so many kinds of distractions, including miracles, made it so difficult to stay focused on the Lord. Whether through the media, those closest to us, substance abuse, trying to do too much too fast, the love of money, being bound by the chains of indebtedness, striving for material possessions, or just the hustle and bustle of everyday routines, the battles to steal, kill, and destroy our relationship with our God and King have never raged hotter. Jesus Himself said, "The thief cometh not, but for to steal, and to kill, and to destroy" (John 10:10). Satan knows full well that his days are numbered and that anyone who presses their way into the secret place will be one less notch that he can carve into his gun stock. Satan hates anything and anyone who brings pleasure to God, and will spare no expense in doing whatever it takes to separate us from Him. If we are going to develop and maintain the ability to live our lives in the presence of God, we are going to have to master the art of staying focused on Him as a lifestyle.

There is a little saying that goes, "Pursuit is the proof of desire." Luke put it this way, "For where your treasure is, there will your heart be also" (Luke 12:34). In other words, what you truly want you will pursue. My dad used to say, "Keith, isn't it amazing how people, no matter how poor or busy, seem to always find the money and/or the time to do what they really want to do." It's just a fact—without the "want to" we will never find our way into the secret place. At any and all cost, we must stay focused on God. Paul addressed this when he said, "Pray without ceasing" (1 Thessalonians 5:17). Contrary to popular belief, this is possible!

Always remember, there is nobody or nothing worth your relationship with God! Peter admonishes us, "But the end of all things is at hand: be ye therefore sober, and watch unto prayer" (1 Peter 4:7). We must be clear-minded and self-controlled so that our communication with God is never interrupted! Failing to reach the secret place is only caused by allowing our focus on God to be broken. We must stay focused!

Thank God that the scriptures lay out an easy-to-understand guideline for anyone who wants to begin and maintain a close relationship with our wonderful God and King. Herein lies the key, "Enter into his gates with thanksgiving, and into his courts with praise: be thankful unto him, and bless his name" (Psalm 100:4). If you study this verse closely, you will see that God has given us a map that, if followed, will lead anyone who desires it straight into the presence of God.

In order to begin our quest to live in the presence of God, we must first learn we are meant to approach Him with hearts filled with thanksgiving! That is totally opposite of the more commonly practiced approach of bringing him a "grocery list" of wants, or throwing ourselves at His feet as a result of some form of problematic hysteria. I'm not saying that we shouldn't bring these things before God. He loves us and is truly concerned with every aspect of our lives. What I am saying is that our problems, wants, or even our needs should never be the first things out of our mouths. If this has been your approach, you need to change it. I can pretty much guarantee that if you were to try to approach an earthly king in that way, it would be considered dreadfully disrespectful and would result in your case not being heard at all. The fact is that with this approach, you would more than likely be forcefully escorted off the castle grounds. If the manner in which one is to approach an earthly king's throne is so important, then wouldn't it stand to reason that the way we approach the throne of the great God and King of the universe is even more important? With any sitting king, there is protocol that must be followed in order to be permitted into their presence, including such things as cleanliness, appropriate speech, and even proper etiquette when exiting a king's presence. It is of extreme importance to know that any deviation from protocol could, as they would say in days of old, cost you your head!

Before we can dwell with God, we must first learn how to approach Him. In order to do this, we must understand that God gave us the example of earthly kings and kingdoms as a way to help us better understand how He designed the Kingdom of Heaven to operate. Our understanding of kingdom protocol is so important to our relating to God that the establishment of kings and kingdoms on the earth played a key role in His timing for sending Jesus to the earth. In order for people to better understand Jesus' teaching about the Kingdom of Heaven, kingdoms had to be established on the earth. This is why I believe Paul said, "But when the fulness of the time was come, God sent forth his Son, made of a woman, made under the law" (Galatians 4:4).

Understanding kingdom life is so important to our relating to God that kings, kingdoms, and other kingdom-related things can be found in over twenty-seven hundred verses in the Bible. I believe that we Christians in America are at a grave disadvantage where understanding kingdom life is concerned. If you have been born and raised here or have lived here for any period of time at all, you know that we are a republic, where most governmental leaders are elected into office. This means that at any given time about half the people in the United States are in favor of the sitting president or government official, while the other half would really rather "hang 'em." I believe that this climate of growing disrespect for leadership has had a crippling effect on how people in this country approach God or view the Church and her leaders! Much like many people in our churches base their views of God on the way their earthly fathers are or were, the same could be said that many Christians in America have based their views on the Kingdom of God by the way they see our government operate, simply because they do not know any better. This is a terrible mistake!

Once we have properly familiarized ourselves with kingdom protocol and have entered God's gates with hearts filled with thanksgiving, our next stop and final destination is His courts, the place where we ultimately stand before our great King. Webster's Dictionary defines "court" or "courts" as "a palace; the place of residence of a king or sovereign prince. The hall, chamber, or place where justice is administered." If we take another look at this scripture in Psalms, it also instructs us on how to enter the place where God Himself resides, His courts. "Enter into his gates with thanksgiving, and into his courts with praise: be thankful unto him, and bless his name" (Psalm 100:4). Once again, the same version of Webster's defines "praise" as "to commend; to applaud; to express approbation (pleasureful approval) of personal worth or actions. To extol in words or song; to magnify; to glorify on account of perfections or excellent works." My favorite account of pure praise for our great God is cited in the book of Revelation:

And the four beasts had each of them six wings about him; and they were full of eyes within: and they rest not day and night, saying, Holy, holy, holy, Lord God Almighty, which was, and is, and is to come. And when those beasts give glory and honor and thanks to him that sat on the throne, who liveth for ever and ever, the four and twenty elders fall down before him that sat on the throne, and worship him that liveth forever and ever, and cast their crowns before the throne, saying, thou art worthy, O Lord, to receive glory and honor and power: for thou hast created all things, and for thy pleasure they are and were created.

Revelation 4:8–11

Praise His wonderful and glorious name! True praise emanates from a "thank-filled" heart and goes up before our Father's throne as a pleasingly sweet-smelling savor. If you have thought, What could I ever do for God?, this would be it! He enjoys nothing more than pure praise from a pure heart! "Sing unto him a new song; play skilfully with a loud noise. For the word of the LORD is right; and all his works are done in truth" (Psalm 33:3–4).

Lastly, at the end of Psalm 100:4, you will notice that once we have entered through His gates and are standing before Him, we are then to bless His name. What does "bless" really mean? The Greek definition of the word bless is "to praise; to celebrate with praise." The Hebrew definition however shows us something a bit different, "to be blessed; to pray to, invoke or to ask a blessing of." The word "invoke" means, "to call forth; to call on for assistance, ask for aid or protection, appeal to someone for help."

Even though God already knows what we need before we ask Him, for the purpose of relationship He still requires that we ask.

> But thou, when thou prayest, enter into thy closet, and when thou hast shut thy door, pray to thy Father which is in secret; and thy Father which seeth in secret shall reward thee openly. But when ye pray, use not vain repetitions, as the heathen do: for they think that they shall be heard for their much speaking. Be not ye therefore like unto them: for your Father knoweth what things ye have need of, before ye ask him.
>
> Matthew 6:6–8

"And it shall come to pass, that before they call, I will answer; and while they are yet speaking, I will hear" (Isaiah 65:24). "Ask, and it shall be given you; seek, and ye shall find; knock, and it shall be opened unto you: For every one that asketh receiveth; and he that seeketh findeth; and to him that knocketh it shall be opened" (Matthew 7:7–8). Never forget, God takes great pleasure in giving to those who truly love and seek Him with all of their hearts! "Delight thyself also in the Lord; and he shall give thee the desires of thine heart" (Psalm 37:4). "If ye abide in me, and my words abide in you, ye shall ask what ye will, and it shall be done unto you" (John 15:7).

Therefore take no thought, saying, What shall we eat? or, What shall we drink? or, Wherewithal shall we be clothed? (For after all these things do the Gentiles seek) for your heavenly Father knoweth that ye have need of all these things. But seek ye first the kingdom of God, and his righteousness; and all these things shall be added unto you.

Matthew 6:31–33

God's Word is clear when He directs us to "enter his gates with thanksgiving and enter his courts with praise: be thankful unto him, and bless his name." Any deviation from this Kingdom protocol will result in our stopping short of a close, loving relationship with God; hence our never truly enjoying His wonderful life or the fulfillment of His perfect will and purpose for our lives. From this day forth I encourage you to make it your lifestyle to take a heart filled with thanksgiving, praises, and blessings before the throne of God, and watch what happens. You will then begin to enjoy the kind of relationship with Him and the kind of fulfillment of His purposes in your life that you have always desired! I guarantee it!

The Cart's before the Horse

I was once approached by a brother in the Lord who told me that he was terribly frustrated with where he was in his walk with God. He went on to tell me that he felt like he should be much further along than he actually was and could not figure out why he could not seem to get any further. When I asked him why he felt the way he did, he said, "I don't know what I'm doing wrong! I'm in church every time the doors are open. I play a regular part in a number of church programs and attend several classes each week. I've cut out watching any bad television shows. I listen to wonderful preachers and teachers on TV, CD, and tape. I study my Bible. I'm eating healthier. I tithe and even give offerings when I am able. And still I feel as if God is nowhere around. Keith, what am I doing wrong?" As I listened to the very lengthy and somewhat noble list of things that he was doing to try to grow in God, it became abundantly obvious that he had left out the most important step of all. He wasn't "diligently seeking" God! Just as so many in the Church have done today, he had fallen into the deadly trap of seeking religion or works instead of a personal relationship with God. He was "in deed" putting "the cart before the horse"!

Don't get me wrong! I am very aware that James teaches us, "Faith without works is dead" (James 2:18). But I also know that James never intended for his profound proclamation to be misinterpreted and used as a wedge to be driven between us and our personal relationship with God Himself. You might ask me, "How can you so readily recognize this ever-growing problem?" Because I have been a chief offender of this very thing myself! You see, I was raised in a home where my dad was a tremendously talented and successful corporate executive who eventually was over the worldwide sales of a Fortune 500 company. Therefore, by a very young age, I had already been acclimated into a bit of a production-oriented mentality, and frankly, I liked it! My dad taught us well "that if any would not work, neither should he eat" (2 Thessalonians 3:10). By the age of twenty-five, I was working as sales manager of a boat dealership where I lived solely on commission. The pressure to produce was intense! If my sales staff didn't sell, guess what? I didn't eat! Until I entered full-time ministry, commission sales was all I had ever known. Even though I enjoy applying many of the things that I have learned in business to making my ministry more effective, I have to continually remind myself that hidden within my strengths lie my greatest weaknesses.

For example, at one point I was working full-time as an outside sales rep for a large Washington, D.C. area printing and graphics firm. At the same time I was pastoring a rather large and growing youth group, playing with the church praise and worship team in four services a week, teaching a Bible school class one night a week at church, holding a Bible study at my home, rehearsing and traveling with my own contemporary music outreach band, periodically promoting large concerts, and counseling folks individually throughout the week, while still having to eat, do my laundry, sleep, and do everything else required in daily living. As much of a desire as I had to serve God and His people, I eventually learned the hard way that even though I might have been doing a lot of good things, I wasn't doing the right thing! Because I was so busy, I seemed to stay in a state of exhaustion. It was because of this state of constant fatigue that I had stopped putting forth the time and the effort needed to seek and spend time with God. And when I did take the time to be alone with Him, my head was spinning so rapidly with everything that I had going on that His voice, when I could hear it, was faint at best. It was also that same fatigue that resulted in my making some pretty bad choices that I would never have made if I had not first allowed myself to wander far away from God and His Word. "How sweet are thy words unto my taste, yea, sweeter than honey to my mouth! Through thy precepts I get understanding: therefore I hate every false way. Thy word is a lamp unto my feet, and a light unto my path" (Psalm 119:103–105).

This is why the vast majority of the Church is in the shape it is in today. People are simply not making time for God! If there has ever been a time when we need to pray for the body of Christ, it is now! Satan's move to distract and separate us from God is escalating rapidly and is resulting in thousands of our precious brothers and sisters in Christ being swept away daily into a miserable lifestyle of busy ineffectiveness—i.e., doing at best good things at the expense of the most important thing! Luke witnessed firsthand possibly the best example in the entire Bible of this very thing when he noted,

> Now it came to pass, as they went, that he entered into a certain village: and a certain woman named Martha received him into her house. And she had a sister called Mary, which also sat at Jesus' feet, and heard his word. But Martha was cumbered about much serving, and came to him, and said, Lord, dost thou not care that my sister hath left me to serve alone? Bid her therefore that she help me. And Jesus answered and said unto her, Martha, Martha, thou art careful and troubled about many things: but one thing is needful: and Mary hath chosen that good part, which shall not be taken away from her.
>
> Luke 10:38–42

Just like Martha, the Church today has become encumbered with many things! In great part, the very institution that is supposed to be raising the standard of intimacy with our Heavenly Father has instead chosen to trample it underfoot in its anxious pursuit of countless numbers of distracting programs, thinking all the while that it is doing God a service. As I heard one preacher say, "Our beloved church has gone from being a living, breathing organism to being a lifeless organization." For example, many church leaders are now choosing to not preach Jesus boldly—fearful that if they do they will offend people, the very people that God has entrusted to them to reach with the uncompromised truth. "And ye shall know the truth, and the truth shall make you free" (John 8:32). There is only one way to reach people, and that is to lift up the wonderful name of Jesus Christ as high as we possibly can!

Jesus gave us the key to effective evangelism when He said, "And I, if I be lifted up from the earth, will draw all men unto me" (John 12:32). What He was saying doesn't only apply to the time of His crucifixion, but also applies just as much today. A pastor friend of mine says, "Sometimes in order to reach a person's heart, you will have to offend their mind!" Sadly enough, the Church in America is "dis-eased," and in many cases dying, simply because it has not put forth the effort to seek Christ diligently! A life without Jesus Christ is in fact no life at all! Jesus says,

> Abide in me, and I in you. As the branch cannot bear
> fruit of itself, except it abide in the vine; no more can
> ye, except ye abide in me. I am the vine, ye are the
> branches: he that abideth in me, and I in him, the
> same bringeth forth much fruit: for without me ye can
> do nothing. If a man abide not in me, he is cast forth

as a branch, and is withered; and men gather them, and cast them into the fire, and they are burned. If ye abide in me, and my words abide in you, ye shall ask what ye will, and it shall be done unto you. Herein is my Father glorified, that ye bear much fruit; so shall ye be my disciples.

John 15:4–8

The sad thing is that thousands of misguided and uninformed people kneel at altars every week at church services across this nation unknowingly professing an allegiance more to a denominational institution or to a leader than to Jesus Christ Himself. "And Jesus answered and said unto them, Take heed that no man deceive you. For many shall come in my name, saying, I am Christ; and shall deceive many" (Matthew 24:4–5). Whenever we take our heart's eye off Jesus, death is soon to follow! "The man that wandereth out of the way of understanding shall remain in the congregation of the dead" (Proverbs 21:16). It is for this very reason that our once Christian nation has now become a stronghold of religion populated in most part by people who at best know about God but don't know Him personally, much less intimately. Paul wrote the following prophecy as a warning concerning this very matter,

This know also, that in the last days perilous times shall come. For men shall be lovers of their own selves, covetous, boasters, proud, blasphemers, disobedient to parents, unthankful, unholy, Without natural affection, trucebreakers, false accusers, incontinent, fierce, despisers of those that are good, Traitors, heady, highminded, lovers of pleasures more than lovers of God; having a form of godliness, but denying the power thereof: from such turn away.

2 Timothy 3:1–5

This trend toward dead religion not only leaves one confused and lifeless, but also holds for those who practice it a very uncomfortable time when eventually facing the judgment seat of Christ.

For other foundation can no man lay than that is laid, which is Jesus Christ. Now if any man build upon this foundation gold, silver, precious stones, wood, hay, stubble; every man's work shall be made manifest: for the day shall declare it, because it shall be revealed by fire; and the fire shall try every man's work of what sort it is. If any man's work abide which he hath built thereupon, he shall receive a reward. If any man's work shall be burned, he shall suffer loss: but he himself shall be saved; yet so as by fire.

1 Corinthians 3:11–15

Many of the works that are going to be burned up are works that looked good in the eyes of men but not in the eyes of God. What makes our works good in the eyes of God? What does it mean to do the will of the Father? Jesus tells us,

Labour not for the meat which perisheth, but for that meat which endureth unto everlasting life, which the Son of man shall give unto you: for him hath God the Father sealed. Then said they unto him, What shall we do, that we might work the works of God? Jesus answered and said unto them, This is the work of God, that ye believe on him whom he hath sent.

John 6:27–29

It is the will of God that we know and love Him intimately! How can we do the will of God if we can't hear His voice? How can a soldier follow an order if he ignores his commanding officer? Paul, writing to the church at Rome, made a profound statement that—I'm sad to say—has been taken out of context in many circles and keeps the Church in this country chained to a "religion over relationship" mentality. He said, "So then faith cometh by hearing, and hearing by the word of God" (Romans 10:17). More often than not, I have heard this scripture used to teach that faith comes by reading the scriptures. As true as that is, it still falls short of what Paul was really wanting us to understand. When he said that "faith cometh by hearing, and hearing by the word of God," he was telling us that "true faith" comes when we actually hear God's voice or spoken word for ourselves! The fact is, we will never be able to fulfill the will of God as individuals or as a body if we are so busy that we don't stop to spend quality time with Him! If we don't spend time with God, we will never hear or know His wonderful voice, and hence, we will not be able to follow Him into His plan and will for our lives.

Jesus heavily emphasized the importance of our being able to hear and know His voice when He said,

> Verily, verily, I say unto you, he that entereth not by the door into the sheepfold, but climbeth up some other way, the same is a thief and a robber. But he that entereth in by the door is the shepherd of the sheep. To him the porter openeth; and the sheep hear his voice: and he calleth his own sheep by name, and leadeth them out. And when he putteth forth his own sheep, he goeth before them, and the sheep follow him: for they know his voice. And a stranger will they not follow, but will flee from him: for they know not the voice of strangers.
>
> John 10:1–5

God loves us and stands ready to bless those who seek Him with all of their hearts! Paul teaches us that God is a rewarder of those who diligently seek Him (Hebrews 11:6). If there is anything or anybody that is hindering you from diligently seeking and spending time with God, I encourage you to make whatever changes are necessary to position yourself at His feet. Always remember that the joy God feels when we lay our accomplishments at His feet will never compare to the joy that He feels when we lay ourselves at His feet! For this reason we should never allow our participation with the platform committee, the choir, the nursery staff, or any other form of church service to come between us and an intimate relationship with God through Jesus Christ! "And now, little children, abide in him; that, when he shall appear, we may have confidence, and not be ashamed before him at his coming" (1 John 2:28).

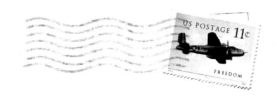

The Fruit's on the End of the Limb

When I was in grade school, I remember vividly the passion that I had for building things, especially tree forts. Each night before we would start to build one—and we built quite a few in those days—I would lie in bed, and my mind would come alive with visions of a tree house second only to the one in Disney's classic movie *The Swiss Family Robinson*. I could see it all so clearly: ladders, trap doors, rope swings, windows, and so much more. I could hardly wait to get home from school the next day to get started on it. As you can imagine, that next day in class was quite a battle for me. It never failed: I would find myself headlong in a fight to stay focused on my schoolwork while at the same time struggling to hold at bay the temptation to daydream about everything I had planned for that afternoon. More often than not, that was a skirmish that regularly ended in my defeat. Once the final bell rang, I would grab my books and head for the bus. It seemed like the bus ride that usually only took about twenty minutes took every bit of an hour. It goes without saying that I could hardly wait to get home!

When I arrived at the bus stop, I and my "buds" would jump off the bus, run home, change into our play clothes, gather up our tools, and head for the woods. Finally, it was time to make the vision a reality!

Anyone who is well-versed in the fine art of tree fort construction will tell you that the first order of business is always the selection of the perfect tree. Living in Virginia Beach at the time, we found that the best trees to build forts in were either maples or oaks. Even though we also had lots of pines, they were not as desirable since their limbs were usually much higher up and rather brittle. Once we selected our tree, we would then locate the materials we needed. Fortunately for us, the housing development where we lived at the time was only a few years old, and was surrounded with quite a few new-home construction sites. We would grab our little red wagons and head straight for the nearest scrap pile. While one guy was picking up discarded nails, others would be digging through the piles for scrap two-by-fours and plywood. Once we had gathered everything we needed, we loaded it all on the wagons and headed for the woods. With our tree picked out and all of the materials together, it was finally time to begin construction.

With our dads' saws and hammers in hand, we went right to work. The first order of business was to cut short pieces of two-by-fours to nail up the trunk of the tree. These would serve as a makeshift ladder. After we nailed them up high enough to reach our desired build spot, it was time to frame up the floor. This was perhaps the most crucial stage of the whole project. Here is how it works. The bigger you want your fort to be, the farther out on the limb you have to go to nail off your first floor supports. So, in reality, the size of your fort is directly related to the courage of the guy whose job it is to make that first trip out on the limb. It is simple: little courage, little tree fort; big courage, big tree fort! After quite a few painful plunges to the ground, I was able to develop a pretty fail-safe method of doing this. I would climb out on the limb until I heard it starting to crack, then I would slide back down the limb about two or three feet and nail the floor support off at that spot. It never failed. That way we knew that we were definitely building the biggest tree fort we could for the size tree we had chosen. It was interesting; we could actually look at the size of some of the other guys' tree forts and tell a lot about their level of courage. Sadly, most of their forts were really nothing more than small platforms nailed very securely to the trunk of their tree. In the dangerous and intimidating world of tree house building, it's just a fact: "scaredy cats" never build big tree forts!

I soon found that the same theory we used for building tree forts also worked nicely when picking apples out of our neighbor's tree. It did not take more than a few seconds to see that the apples did not grow out of the trunk of the tree, and that if we wanted to enjoy them, we were going to have to go out on the end of the limb to get them. Sure, you can cling to the trunk where it is much safer, and occasionally reach far enough to grab an apple or two; but if you really want an abundant harvest, you will have to go out on the limb. This is not a task for the fainthearted. The whole time you are out there, you are faced with two thoughts: first, just how good the apples are going to taste once you get out to them; and second, just how far it will be to the ground if you fall. I eventually learned that the more I would venture out on limbs, the less I would fall or even worry about falling.

When was the last time you "went out on a limb"—or as we Christians say, "stepped out in faith"—for something to the point of actually hearing the limb cracking under you? For some, it could be getting the courage to share your love for Jesus with unbelievers; for someone else, it could be asking their boss for a much-needed promotion; or for others it could be getting the courage to leave a church that is steeped in religion to pursue one that practices the entire Word of God. No matter what they are pursuing, the sound of "the limb cracking" means different things to different people. To most, that sound represents impending doom that usually results in their despairing of ever reaching their goals in life. To the rare few who really trust God, that cracking sound is always an indication that abundance lies just up ahead.

While working in the corporate world, I had a little saying that I would use in our sales meetings, "The risk takers eventually become the money makers!" That same principle also applies to our life in Christ. If we truly want to live the abundant life that Jesus came to provide for us, we are simply going to have to turn loose of life's trunk, or the place of comfort in our lives, and climb out to where the fruit is. "I am come that they might have life, and that they might have it more abundantly" (John 10:10). As noted earlier, we refer to this process of going out on the limb as "stepping out in faith," and if we are going to be successful as Christians, walking by faith is going to have to become our life. Here is a little secret: successful Christians live what unsuccessful Christians only do occasionally! "For we walk by faith, not by sight" (2 Corinthians 5:7). As a matter of fact, walking by faith is not simply an option, it is mandatory if we want to be pleasing to God! Paul teaches us, "But without faith it is impossible to please him [God]: for he that cometh to God must believe that he is, and that he is a rewarder of them that diligently seek him" (Hebrews 11:6). How can we ever expect God to reward us if we are not a pleasure to Him? If we are ever going to be successful in God's eyes, we must make stepping out in faith our way of life. He just loves to watch us climb out on life's limbs!

In all the Bible, perhaps the most publicized account of someone going out on a limb to please God was that of Abraham in Genesis. Think about it for a moment. After Abraham had waited decades to finally have a son, God then required of Abraham that he sacrifice his son.

And it came to pass after these things, that God did tempt Abraham, and said unto him, Abraham: and he said, Behold, here I am. And he said, Take now thy son, thine only son Isaac, whom thou lovest, and get thee into the land of Moriah; and offer him there for a burnt offering upon one of the mountains which I will tell thee of. And Abraham rose up early in the morning, and saddled his ass, and took two of his young men with him, and Isaac his son, and clave the wood for the burnt offering, and rose up, and went unto the place of which God had told him. Then on the third day Abraham lifted up his eyes, and saw the place afar off. And Abraham said unto his young men, Abide ye here with the ass; and I and the lad will go yonder and worship, and come again to you. And Abraham took the wood of the burnt offering, and laid it upon Isaac his son; and he took the fire in his hand, and a knife; and they went both of them together. And Isaac spake unto Abraham his father, and said, My father: and he said, Here am I, my son. And he said, Behold the fire and the wood: but where is the lamb for a burnt offering? And Abraham said, My son, God will provide himself a lamb for a burnt offering: so they went both of them together. And they came to the place which God had told him of; and Abraham built an altar there, and laid the wood in order, and bound Isaac his son, and laid him on the altar upon the wood. And Abraham stretched forth his hand, and took the knife to slay his son. And the angel of the LORD called unto him out of heaven, and said, Abraham, Abraham: and he said, Here am I. And he said, Lay not thine hand upon the lad, neither do thou any thing unto him: for now I know that thou fearest God, seeing thou hast not withheld thy son, thine only son from me. And Abraham lifted up his eyes, and looked, and behold behind him a ram caught in a thicket by his horns: and Abraham went and took the ram, and offered him up for a burnt offering in the stead of his son. And Abraham called the name of that place Jehovahjireh: as it is said to this day, In the mount of the Lord it shall be seen. And the angel of the Lord called unto Abraham out of heaven the second time, And said, By myself have I sworn, saith the Lord, for because thou hast done this thing, and hast not withheld thy son, thine only son: That in blessing I will bless thee, and in multiplying I will multiply thy seed as the stars of the heaven, and as the sand which is upon the sea shore; and thy seed shall possess the gate of his enemies; And in thy seed shall all the nations of the earth be blessed; because thou hast obeyed my voice.

Genesis 22:1–18

Be perfectly honest, after waiting years for the fulfillment of your dream, do you really think you could sacrifice it for the sake of being obedient to God? Do you personally know and love God enough to trust Him that much? If not, you will always find yourself clinging to the fruitless trunk of life's tree where abundance will continually be just out of reach for you. Faith is the basis of everything where God is concerned, and frankly, those who do not trust Him will always live just outside of a fulfilled life. Ironically, this is where the vast majority of folks who claim to be Christians dwell. The Church today is filled with hearers of God's Word, but it possesses very few doers. "But be ye doers of the word, and not hearers only, deceiving your own selves" (James 1:22).

The unsaved world, whether they know it or not, is looking for someone who will lead the way into life's fulfillment, and that someone is supposed to be you and I. "For the earnest expectation of the creature waiteth for the manifestation of the sons of God" (Romans 8:19). Both the unsaved world and the Church today are in desperate need of godly heroes. What this means for you and me is that we now have the priceless opportunity to both model and speak God's Word to this lost and rapidly dying generation.

What part has God called you to play in this end times harvest of souls? Can you say without a shadow of a doubt that you are doing everything that you possibly can to see that calling fulfilled in your life? It's time to trust God's Word, be saturated with it, and be transformed by it so that you may obey it! Only after you do that will you taste the sweetness of good success.

This book of the law shall not depart out of thy mouth; but thou shalt meditate therein day and night, that thou mayest observe to do according to all that is written therein: for then thou shalt make thy way prosperous, and then thou shalt have good success.

Joshua 1:8

Next to Abraham offering up Isaac, possibly the most widely-publicized account of someone stepping out in faith was that of Peter.

> But the ship was now in the midst of the sea, tossed with waves: for the wind was contrary. And in the fourth watch of the night Jesus went unto them, walking on the sea. And when the disciples saw him walking on the sea, they were troubled, saying, It is a spirit; and they cried out for fear. But straightway Jesus spake unto them, saying, Be of good cheer; it is I; be not afraid. And Peter answered him and said, Lord, if it be thou, bid me come unto thee on the water. And he said, Come. And when Peter was come down out of the ship, he walked on the water, to go to Jesus.
>
> Matthew 14:24–29

Sure, Peter started to sink after a while, but who else in the boat loved and trusted Jesus enough to even try to walk on water? Never forget, it is always better to have tried and failed than to have never tried!

If we never climb out there, we will never eat of the fruit of abundance! Think about it for a moment. Who else do you know that can actually say that they have walked on water? Can you imagine how God feels when we believe Him enough to attempt something that we have never before had the courage to try? Much like the jubilation that occurs between parents at the sight of their child taking its first steps, God also rejoices when we, His children, attempt to step out in His Word, like Peter. You must understand, Peter was okay as long as he maintained his focus on Jesus. His problems began as soon as he took his eyes off Christ and put them on the circumstances that surrounded him.

Is there something you are praying for that has not yet come to pass? Is there something that you have been wanting to do, but have not attempted yet? I encourage you to throw off any fears or doubts you may have, and seek God for guidance. Launch out into the deep in faith, keeping your eyes on the Lord, and Jesus will bless you in the same way that He blessed Peter and the guys for their obedience to His commands!

> Now when he [Jesus] had left speaking, he said unto Simon, Launch out into the deep, and let down your nets for a draught. And Simon answering said unto him, Master, we have toiled all the night, and have taken nothing: nevertheless at thy word I will let down the net. And when they had this done, they inclosed a great multitude of fishes: and their net brake. And they beckoned unto their partners, which were in the other ship, that they should come and help them. And they came, and filled both the ships, so that they began to sink.
>
> Luke 5:4–7

This is the same kind of abundance that God has in store for any of us who are obedient to act on His

Word! Look again at what resulted from Abraham's obedience to God's assignment for his life.

> And the angel of the LORD called unto Abraham out of heaven the second time, And said, By myself have I sworn, saith the Lord, for because thou hast done this thing, and hast not withheld thy son, thine only son: That in blessing I will bless thee, and in multiplying I will multiply thy seed as the stars of the heaven, and as the sand which is upon the sea shore; and thy seed shall possess the gate of his enemies; And in thy seed shall all the nations of the earth be blessed; because thou hast obeyed my voice.
>
> Genesis 22:15–18

Think about that! Because of Abraham's obedience, all nations have been blessed!

Not only will we suffer when we fail to act on God's Word and assignment for our lives, but many others will suffer through our disobedience. Be courageous, be strong, throw back your shoulders, and walk right into the face of the intimidating spirits that have, in the past, hindered you from possessing the fulfillment of God's promises for your life. And never forget, "When thou passest through the waters, I will be with thee; and through the rivers, they shall not overflow thee: when thou walkest through the fire, thou shalt not be burned; neither shall the flame kindle upon thee." (Isaiah 43:2)

I encourage you with all of my heart to regularly set aside a time to pray and fast for the purpose of hearing God's voice for your life's assignments. If I had not faced my own fear of climbing trees, my friends and I would have never enjoyed playing in the nicest tree forts or eating the sweetest fruit. The word that the Lord has given me for you is this:

> Enlarge the place of thy tent, and let them stretch forth the curtains of thine habitations: spare not, lengthen thy cords, and strengthen thy stakes; For thou shalt break forth on the right hand and on the left; and thy seed shall inherit the Gentiles, and make the desolate cities to be inhabited.
>
> Isaiah 54:2–3

God has so much more for you, and it is time to get out there. Believe me, what you find will bless you beyond measure! "I can do all things through Christ which strengtheneth me" (Philippians 4:13). That means you!

The Rarest of All Breeds!

Over the years I have watched several documentaries on television concerning various breeds of animals from around the world that many claim are nearing extinction. These documentaries are produced by people who believe very strongly that we are currently experiencing a steep decline in the numbers of some of our planet's rarest breeds of critters due to many reasons, including the destruction of their habitats resulting from new construction, hunting for sport, or poaching. Now, before you begin forming the opinion that I have become, as I have heard them called, one of those tree huggin', animals rights wackos, please hear me out!

The body of Christ has its self-seeking, fringe extremists who have in many ways tarnished the reputation of the truly faithful. Likewise, if you were to press through the more publicly visible and usually immature fringe members of the animal preservation efforts, I'm pretty sure you will find at its core a truly dedicated group of people who are committed not to the acquisition of public recognition but the earnest well being of the animals that they are trying to save.

"A righteous man regardeth the life of his beast: but the tender mercies of the wicked are cruel" (Proverbs 12:10). God is very proud of His animals, and if it were not for these people looking after them, there is no telling what abuses they might suffer.

These small groups of devoted individuals, and not the self-seeking extremists, are responsible for the progress being made in restoring these wonderful animals. The hard work and devotion of organizations like Steve Irwin's Australia Zoo means the next generation will be able to enjoy seeing these animals in the wild and will also reap the benefits of the crucial part that each of them plays in the balance of our planet's highly sophisticated ecosystem.

We must understand that God is a God of purpose and that everything that He does is and was intricately designed and produced to fulfill a specific part in His overall plan! This plan was enacted before the very foundation of the earth was even laid. When just one piece in His plan has been removed or tampered with, the ripple effect eventually impacts all of us in one way or another. Paul teaches us,

> For the earnest expectation of the creature waiteth for the manifestation of the sons of God. For the creature was made subject to vanity, not willingly, but by reason of him who hath subjected the same in hope, Because the creature itself also shall be delivered from the bondage of corruption into the glorious liberty of the

children of God. For we know that the whole creation groaneth and travaileth in pain together until now.

Romans 8:19–22

If something exists, you can rest assured that it has both been well thought out and assigned a crucial role to play in this most intricate of all chess games. God never has and never will make a mistake. If something or someone exists, there is a specific reason!

Just as God has designed and fashioned everything on this planet to play a very important role in the balance of the earth, He has also designed and provided key elements to ensure the proper balance, growth, and advancement of the Church of Jesus Christ! "Having predestinated us unto the adoption of children by Jesus Christ to himself, according to the good pleasure of his will, To the praise of the glory of his grace, wherein he hath made us accepted in the beloved" (Ephesians 1:5–6).

Paul, in his letter to the Ephesians, lays out these provisions in the form of what the Church refers to as the five-fold ministry. "And he gave some, apostles; and some, prophets; and some, evangelists; and some, pastors and teachers; for the perfecting of the saints, for the work of the ministry, for the edifying of the body of Christ" (Ephesians 4:11–12). Remove or tamper with any of these offices and the balance of this very intricate system will not just hinder God's plan and purpose for us today, but the ripple effects will also cripple the church in the future.

Although thousands upon thousands of books have been written on each one of the offices of the five-fold ministry, I would like to take this opportunity to share with you what I have personally found over the years to be not only the rarest but the most important office of them all, "The selfless servant!"

When God designed the five-fold ministry, I can assure you that He never intended for any of these offices to serve as a means by which one could obtain, for selfish reasons, a position of prominence within the Church and community. On the contrary, it has always been His original purpose and design for these most important of positions to be occupied only by people who are first and foremost "selfless servants" at heart, people whose passion it is to see the hearts of others come to the saving knowledge of Jesus Christ and then proceed into God's very best for their lives. If this is not one's sole purpose for being in the ministry, then they would be well advised to back away from it and rethink their motives before continuing any further. Jesus teaches us, "Verily, verily, I say unto you, He that entereth not by the door into the sheepfold, but climbeth up some other way, the same is a thief and a robber. But he that entereth in by the door is the shepherd of the sheep" (John 10:1–2). If you notice, Jesus said, "He that entereth not by the door into the sheepfold, but climbeth up some other way, the same is a thief and a robber."

What does He mean when He says "the door"? Where is this door? Several verses later in this same chapter Jesus very clearly explains the point that He was making.

> Then said Jesus unto them again, Verily, verily, I say unto you, I am the door of the sheep. All that ever came before me are thieves and robbers: but the sheep did not hear them. I am the door: by me if any man enter in, he shall be saved, and shall go in and out, and find pasture. The thief cometh not, but for to steal, and to kill, and to destroy: I am come that they might have life, and that they might have it more abundantly. I am the good shepherd: the good shepherd giveth his life for the sheep. But he that is an hireling, and not the shepherd, whose own the sheep are not, seeth the wolf coming, and leaveth the sheep, and fleeth: and the wolf catcheth them, and scattereth the sheep. The hireling fleeth, because he is an hireling, and careth not for the sheep. I am the good shepherd, and know my sheep, and am known of mine. As the Father knoweth me, even so know I the Father: and I lay down my life for the sheep.
>
> John 10:7–15

What is the door for the sheep? Jesus Christ! Where is the door? It is found only as we are transformed into the image of Christ Himself. For in so doing we develop the same love for people that Jesus has!

The only correct way to pursue serving both God and His people is to approach it in the same way that Jesus does, with an all-consuming love for everyone, no matter who they are, what they can do for you, or what they have done in life, good or bad! Before we can even begin to walk in this same kind of selfless love for others, we must first die to our own selfish wants and desires! "Verily, verily, I say unto you, Except a corn of wheat fall into the ground and die, it abideth alone: but if it die, it bringeth forth much fruit. He that loveth his life shall lose it; and he that hateth his life in this world shall keep it unto life eternal" (John 12:24–25).

> And he [Jesus] came to Capernaum: and being in the house he asked them, What was it that ye disputed among yourselves by the way? But they held their peace: for by the way they had disputed among themselves, who should be the greatest. And he [Jesus] sat down, and called the twelve, and saith unto them, If any man desire to be first, the same shall be last of all, and servant of all.
>
> Mark 9:33–35

This scripture must be etched in the hearts of all who aspire to function within the realm of God's love and service. If it is not, then we are really no better than the hirelings that Jesus spoke of in John 10. "Then said Jesus unto his disciples, If any man will come after me, let him deny himself, and take up his cross, and follow me. For whosoever will save his life shall lose it: and whosoever will lose his life for my sake shall find it" (Matthew 16:24–25). Those who are out for themselves and not out for the fulfillment of God's vision will always function within the confines of lifeless religion.

Whether we realize it or not, there are two versions of ministry. One operates by the power of the Holy Spirit and the other is the terribly distorted version fueled by the arm of flesh. This is the principle difference between God's ministry and man's plans. "There are many devices in a man's heart; nevertheless the counsel of the Lord, that shall stand" (Proverbs 19:21). If you struggle with not being able to tell the difference between the two, all you have to do is watch to see whether or not they truly love both God and people. God's ministry and ministers are always totally focused on the well being of people, while man's devices are for the most part focused on doing things that bring them recognition in the eyes of their peers and overseers—these people are driven by how they are perceived.

Much like liberal politicians will watch various polls to determine their next plan of action, "religious" leaders will take their marching orders from the opinions of congregational members rather than God Himself. Note: there is also a flip side to this. There are those who seek to control peoples' opinions by giving burdensome marching orders and thereby keeping the people so busy "doing" that they never accomplish the "being." If love is not the motive for all we do, then what we do, no matter how good it seems, will always be done at the expense of what is right! Jesus said, "A new commandment I give unto you, That ye love one another; as I have loved you, that ye also love one another. By this shall all men know that ye are my disciples, if ye have love one to another" (John 13:34–35). Love, first for God and then for people, is the key for a life of Christ-like service.

> Jesus said unto him, Thou shalt love the Lord thy God with all thy heart, and with all thy soul, and with all thy mind. This is the first and great commandment. And the second is like unto it, Thou shalt love thy neighbour as thyself. On these two commandments hang all the law and the prophets.
>
> Matthew 22:37–40

Therefore, if all the law and the prophets hang on love, then without love whatever we do is futile. Paul teaches us this in his letter to the Corinthians,

> Though I speak with the tongues of men and of angels, and have not charity, I am become as sounding brass, or a tinkling cymbal. And though I have the gift of prophecy, and understand all mysteries, and all knowledge; and though I have all faith, so that I could remove mountains, and have not charity, I am nothing. And though I bestow all my goods to feed the poor, and though I give my body to be burned, and have not charity, it profiteth me nothing.
>
> 1 Corinthians 13:1–3

On the same subject, John wrote,

If a man say, I love God, and hateth his brother, he is a liar: for he that loveth not his brother whom he hath seen, how can he love God whom he hath not seen? And this commandment have we from him, that he who loveth God love his brother also.

1 John 4:20–21

If love is not the foundation on which we build our lives and ministries, then we have totally missed what Jesus has been trying to teach us all along—speaking in tongues, prophesying, and doing mighty works that seem miraculous are nothing without the love of God. Doing such things does not even mean a person is saved!

Not every one that saith unto me, Lord, Lord, shall enter into the kingdom of heaven; but he that doeth the will of my Father which is in heaven. Many will say to me in that day, Lord, Lord, have we not prophesied in thy name? and in thy name have cast out devils? and in thy name done many wonderful works? And then will I profess unto them, I never knew you: depart from me, ye that work iniquity.

Matthew 7:21–23

Think about it for a moment: a guest preacher comes to speak at your church one Sunday morning. About halfway through the service, he steps down off the platform and walks over to a middle-aged lady sitting in a wheelchair that you and everyone else in the service has known to be crippled since birth. When he gets over to her, he places his hand on the top of her head and, with an authority the likes of which you have never seen before, shouts, "Woman, arise!" All of a sudden, the lady jumps up out of her wheelchair and begins to run around the sanctuary. Now, most would probably draw the immediate conclusion that this guy must be in pretty good standing with God if he can go around doing things like that. This is not necessarily true. What Jesus was teaching us in the previous scripture reveals the tremendously important fact that just because someone performs miraculous feats does in no way indicate that they even have a personal relationship with Jesus.

> Even him, whose coming is after the working of Satan with all power and signs and lying wonders, And with all deceivableness of unrighteousness in them that perish; because they received not the love of the truth, that they might be saved. And for this cause God shall send them strong delusion, that they should believe a lie: That they all might be damned who believed not the truth, but had pleasure in unrighteousness.
>
> 2 Thessalonians 2:9–12

Sadly, the church has become in large part filled with people who have never been taught this. It is as if it has always been taken for granted that miracles are simply an indicator or proof of God's favor on someone's life.

This frame of thought could not be further from the truth!

Now Peter and John went up together into the temple at the hour of prayer, being the ninth hour. And a certain man lame from his mother's womb was carried, whom they laid daily at the gate of the temple which is called Beautiful, to ask alms of them that entered into the temple; who seeing Peter and John about to go into the temple asked an alms. And Peter, fastening his eyes upon him with John, said, Look on us. And he gave heed unto them, expecting to receive something of them. Then Peter said, Silver and gold have I none; but such as I have give I thee: In the name of Jesus Christ of Nazareth rise up and walk. And he took him by the right hand, and lifted him up: and immediately his feet and ankle bones received strength. And he leaping up stood, and walked, and entered with them into the temple, walking, and leaping, and praising God. And all the people saw him walking and praising God: And they knew that it was he which sat for alms at the Beautiful gate of the temple: and they were filled with wonder and amazement at that which had happened unto him. And as the lame man which was healed held Peter and John, all the people ran together unto them in the porch that is called Solomon's, greatly wondering. And when Peter saw it, he answered unto the people, Ye men of Israel, why marvel ye at this? or why look ye so earnestly on us, as though by our own power or holiness we had made this man to walk?

Acts 3:1–12

True servants of God are always aware of the fact that they are simply working with God to perform His will and purpose! Much like a gardener uses a garden hose to transfer water from a water source to his garden, we as servants of the most high God are called to perform much the same task, bringing His love to those around us. When we introduce "self" into the picture, it is like the gardener disconnecting the hose. It disrupts the flow of God's love in and through our lives. "For it is God which worketh in you both to will and to do of his good pleasure" (Philippians 2:13).

The Apostle Paul, discussing the "self" issue writes,

For I know that in me (that is, in my flesh) dwelleth no good thing: for to will is present with me; but how to perform that which is good I find not. For the good that I would I do not: but the evil which I would not, that I do. Now if I do that I would not, it is no more I that do it, but sin that dwelleth in me. I find then a law, that, when I would do good, evil is present with me. For I delight in the law of God after the inward man: But I see another law in my members, warring against the law of my mind, and bringing me into captivity to the law of sin which is in my members. O wretched man that I am! who shall deliver me from the body of this death? I thank God through Jesus

Christ our Lord. So then with the mind I myself serve the law of God; but with the flesh the law of sin.

Romans 7:18–25

If we have a bunch of gardeners in the church who do not have their garden hoses connected to the water source, it will result in fruitlessness. God said, "For my people have committed two evils; they have forsaken me the fountain of living waters, and hewed them out cisterns, broken cisterns, that can hold no water" (Jeremiah 2:13). I believe that is the reason that we are now living in a time where Satan and self-seeking church folk have pretty much conditioned the general population to avoid, at all costs, involvement with anything that remotely resembles the Church of Jesus Christ.

Phrases like "all they want is my money" and "they're all just a bunch of hypocrites" are being wielded as a means by which they conveniently remain in their sin while attempting to justify not being or ever becoming involved with the body of Christ in any capacity. This is where we come in! If you know folks who have made a bold stand against the things of God, then wrap the things of God in love and give this to them with a smile. Get creative, pick up the phone, or write them a letter letting them know that you care and that God cares. I have found over the years that the phone company, the United States Postal Service, and the Internet provide three of the most effective means by which we can daily spread the love of Jesus to people. The age-old belief that it is the pastor and his staff's job to do all of the work of the ministry has created in the church today the equivalent of a welfare state. This demonic revelation that has been forged in the minds of many Christians—that the giving of their tithes and offerings somehow releases them from service—has greatly diminished the Church's effectiveness where spreading the love of Jesus Christ is concerned. Don't buy it! "And he [God] gave some, apostles; and some, prophets; and some, evangelists; and some, pastors and teachers; for the perfecting of the saints, for the work of the ministry, for the edifying of the body of Christ" (Ephesians 4:11–12). It is time that we all throw off any preconceived misconception of what ministry should be, gird ourselves with the towel of loving service, and be counted among the ranks of the selfless servants!

Three Keys to God-Pleasing Faith

In the late '80s, I was serving as youth pastor over a rather large and growing group of young people for a church on the outskirts of Washington, D.C. During the same period of time, I was also holding down a full time job as an outside sales representative for a commercial printing and graphics firm, playing on the church praise and worship team five services a week, teaching a Bible class one night a week at the church, conducting a Bible study at my home one night a week, attending early morning prayer six mornings a week at the church, promoting large Christian rock concerts, plus rehearsing and playing with my own music outreach band. This was in addition to doing the usual activities like eating, sleeping, and maintaining a household. Unbeknownst to me, I was well on my way to possessing a terrible case of fatigue. If there was a silver lining around that cloud at all it was that I learned the valuable and costly lesson that when we are fatigued, molehills become mountains and we become most vulnerable to attack. Webster's Dictionary defines the word "vulnerable" as "that can be wounded or injured," "open to, or easily hurt by, criticism or attack." It was in this state of vulnerability that I arrived at a place of utter frustration.

During a Sunday evening service on a cold January night, it caught up with me. After the praise team finished its portion of the service and we were making our way to our seats, it hit me. I felt as if I had been completely drained of energy. I was soon overcome with flu-like symptoms and a deep anguish that caused me to do something that I had not done in at least five years—I left the service early. As I went to the car, all I could think was that I wanted to be alone. I drove home, stumbled through the front door, and collapsed into the living room chair. After sitting there for several minutes, I grabbed the television remote and turned the TV on to watch one of the more well-known preachers of the time. This particular night he was speaking on faith, and with what I was going through, I quickly poised myself to hang onto every word that he had to say. I desperately needed a word from God! As I listened to him, I noticed that there was something not quite right with his message, but I could not put my finger on just what it was. All of a sudden it dawned on me! As good of a job as he did, I noticed that he had just spent an entire hour preaching on how we can't please God without faith, but he failed to explain how we as believers can obtain it. Talk about adding insult to injury! There I was, going through perhaps the toughest time of my life, desperately needing a word from God, and nothin', zilch, nada!

I turned the television off and went down the hall to my bedroom. As I got ready for bed, I reflected on what the TV preacher just shared, while the grief that I was already feeling increased substantially. I sat on the edge of my bed, turned the light off, put my head in my hands, and began to weep. I was in a state of total brokenness. I slid off my bed onto my knees and cried out to God, praying "Father, if it is impossible to please you without faith, then please help me to find the handle on the kind of faith that makes you happy. All I want is to know that I am pleasing you!" What happened next would change my life! With my face now buried in the carpet and my ear desperately tuned to hearing the voice of the Lord, it happened!

The Lord's presence filled the room, and with a clarity unlike I had ever heard Him speak before, He said, "Sit up, I have come to answer your prayer." After I sat up, He said, "I am here to explain to you how to obtain the kind of faith that makes me happy!" It was then that, in the Spirit, He placed His hand on my back and ushered me straight up through the ceiling of my bedroom, through the attic, and through the roof of the house. We proceeded upward into the night sky to about fifteen hundred feet over my neighborhood.

Even though it was the dead of winter at the time, I clearly remember not being affected in the least by the frigid temperature. It is extremely difficult to explain. It was as if there was no climate whatsoever; the comfort level was indefinable. I remember passing through the attic of my house and seeing the rafters and insulation vividly. I remember looking down as we ascended upward and seeing the cars with their headlights on traveling up and down the streets of my neighborhood. In that one swift instance, every great thing that I had ever heard or read about the awesomeness of God was exceeded immeasurably. Even the phrase, "I couldn't put it into words" was a vast understatement! Once we reached His desired height, He positioned us, like a helicopter would hover, directly over the main entrance to the neighborhood. It was there that He would answer my prayer and give me the three keys to God-pleasing faith.

Before I attempt to explain in the best way I know how what words were not designed to describe, I would like to lay just a bit more groundwork for you. I did not know it at the time, but He had taken me over the entrance of my neighborhood because there were three roads from that entrance that led to my house. It would be these three roads that He would use as a map to help me understand how to obtain the faith that I so desired.

As we were suspended over the entrance of the neighborhood, He leaned over to me and said, "Son, do you see your house in the distance?"

I said, "Yes, Lord."

He said, "We are going to pretend that your house is your desired destination of the kind of faith that brings me joy." He then asked, "Do you see the main road below you that leads into your community?"

I said, "Yes, Lord."

He said, "We are going to call this road, 'You Must Learn How to Trust in Me Boulevard'." He then asked, "Do you see the road just up ahead on the left that leads over to the street your house is on?"

I said, "Yes, Lord."

He said, "We are going to call that road, 'You Must Learn How to Rest in Me Street'." He then asked, "Do you see the road that leads up to your house?"

I said, "Yes, Lord."

He said, "We will call it, 'You Must Learn How to Wait on Me Drive'." He then said, "Do you see now, if you get on 'You Must Learn How to Trust in Me Boulevard,' make a left on 'You Must Learn How to Rest in Me Street', and then make a right on to 'You Must Learn How to Wait on Me Drive', you will, at the end of that road, find the kind of faith that makes Me happy! Once you learn how to trust in Me, rest in Me, and wait on Me, you will have obtained the kind of faith that fills My heart with unspeakable joy. These are the three key ingredients to God-pleasing faith." As soon as He said that, I found myself instantaneously back on the floor in my bedroom.

As you can imagine, at that point all I could do was offer up songs of gratitude and praise, and even that seemed so insufficient in the presence of the Almighty King of all kings. Again, what I experienced is hard to express with mere words! After about fifteen minutes, I laid prostrate on the floor to wait on Him once again. As I was quietly lying there listening for Him, He spoke for the second time. This time it was in the form of a stern warning. He said, "Never forget, the archenemy to the kind of faith that pleases Me is the demonic spirit of anxiousness, gird yourself against it!"

Immediately understanding washed over me! I saw so plainly the reason why so many people were being herded into the frustrating throes of dead religion. Many people walk around having a form of godliness but without the power. They rely solely on self-sufficiency—the arm of flesh—rather than taking the time and effort necessary to acquire true faith in God, the ability to trust, rest, and wait totally on Him in every situation. Now I understand better what Paul meant when he said,

> This know also, that in the last days perilous times shall come. For men shall be lovers of their own selves, covetous, boasters, proud, blasphemers, disobedient to parents, unthankful, unholy, Without natural affection, trucebreakers, false accusers, incontinent, fierce, despisers of those that are good, traitors, heady, highminded, lovers of pleasures more than lovers of God; having a form of godliness, but denying the power thereof: from such turn away.
>
> 2 Timothy 3:1–5

Paul was simply warning us to stay away from anyone or anything that would hinder our obtaining the ability to "*trust, rest, and wait*" on God!

Up to that point in my walk with the Lord, I must admit to you that I did not have a very good understanding of what faith really was, and frankly, neither did most of the people with whom I had discussed the subject. Plenty of folks seemed to know the consequences of not having faith, but nobody knew how to get it. Just about all of the teachings that I had heard or read on the subject were vague at best using as the basis for their teaching Paul's brief explanation of faith in Hebrews, "Now faith is the substance of things hoped for, the evidence of things not seen" (Hebrews 11:1). As wonderful a job as Paul did explaining what he knew faith to be, I still could not quite grasp what he meant. Sure, I was pretty well familiar with most of the popular buzz phrases of the day, but when it came right down to it, the real definition of faith was at best a gray area to most. Even though, after an exhaustive search, I could not find a clear definition of faith anywhere in the scriptures, I eventually came to the realization that I did not need to have faith defined in order to have it operating in my life. During that same period of time, the faith message became so misrepresented that I found myself beginning to sidestep the issue whenever it arose. The whole "faith thing" was no more than the password for a growing group of people who worshipped it for what it could do for them personally rather than worshipping God Himself. The faith message was really no more than the teaching of cranked-up or turbo-charged hope.

Even those who were teaching the more balanced faith message of the day were being taken way out of context by the rapidly growing sect of the self seeking. For example, I recall hearing Dr. Kenneth Hagin, a precious minister of the gospel who has now gone on to be with the Lord, tell of a time when he and a group of his colleagues were having dinner at a nearby restaurant after one of his meetings. As they were eating, they overheard a group of people sitting at a table that was on the other side of a partition from them. These folks had obviously attended the meeting and were recapping things that Brother Hagin had taught on that night. Brother Hagin said that he was shocked as he overheard these people telling each other what they heard Brother Hagin say, things that Brother Hagin knew that he never said. He later added, "No wonder the faith message was coming under such intense scrutiny!" You see, when someone listens to what you are saying, it doesn't mean they hear or understand what you say!

For instance, in 1982 I spent quite a bit of time during the summer waterskiing with a new friend and his wife, both of whom were steeped in the teachings of the unbalanced faith movement. They both worked as managers with a large corporation and were very wealthy. They had the palatial home, nice cars, good looks, and everything else that society deems successful. One day he called me and said he was having problems with his teeth and had been advised to see a dentist. Not quite convinced in his heart that God was going to supernaturally heal him, he called me in hopes that I would say, "You don't need to go to a dentist; just believe God for your healing!" I did in fact tell him to believe God for healing, but I also added that I felt that, to be safe, he should go ahead and at least see what a dentist had to say.

As soon as I suggested that to him, he became a bit angry with me and replied, "Well, I'll just have to pray about that!" He then hung up the phone, and I didn't hear back from him for several days. To make a long story short, due to an increase in his pain, he eventually went to the dentist. They did a much-needed surgical procedure, and he was well on his way to receiving the healing that he so desperately needed even though it was not happening the way that he had hoped. Because the dentist had to make several incisions as a part of his surgery, an antibiotic was prescribed to ward off any possible infection that might occur. The doctor specifically instructed him to take one of the pills every eight hours until the entire bottle was gone. Two days later, he was given a tape on divine healing by someone from his church. After listening to the tape, against my advice and the advice of others, he took the antibiotics and flushed them down the toilet and said, "I don't receive this infection." A minister friend later told me that the infection soon spread throughout his entire mouth to the point of his having to have almost half of his lower jaw removed.

My friend was not walking by faith at all. He and many others in the so-called Faith Movement are walking by revved-up false hope instead of by faith, and they are actually violating the scripture that says, "Thou shalt not tempt the Lord thy God" (Matthew 4:7). If we attempt to imitate faith in the flesh, we cannot expect God's power to be the result. Had my friend truly been walking in faith, he would have sought God's will on the matter and obeyed Him. Just as Peter did not leap out of the boat and attempt to walk on water until Jesus called Him, so also should we not leap out unless God has truly called us to do so. When God does call us to do something, we can rest assured He has made every provision for us. That is when it is time for faith and works to be made perfect together.

For example, suppose you want a beautiful green lawn for the summer. You made your request known to God. He, working through an anonymous donor, supernaturally provides the money for your fertilizer, grass seed, and the necessary tools to get the job done. How nice do you think your lawn will look when spring comes, if all you have done is purchased the materials and equipment, while refusing to do the work needed to get the seed and fertilizer out of the bags and into the ground? You're right, you will have the same old brown tumbleweed lookin' mess you have had for the past several years, simply because you didn't put feet on your faith and get the work done.

James teaches us, "Even so faith, if it hath not works, is dead, being alone. Yea, a man may say, Thou hast faith, and I have works: shew me thy faith without thy works, and I will shew thee my faith by my works" (James 2:17–18). Combine the two, faith and works, and you will be well on your way to bringing a smile to the face of God!

Now, let's take a moment and look at each of the three keys that make up God-pleasing faith. The first key is *trust*. What is trust? The Hebrew word for trust is "batach" (Strong's Exhaustive Concordance). It expresses that sense of well-being and security which results from having something or someone in whom to place confidence, to trust, be confident or sure; be bold (confident, secure, sure) careless, put confidence, (make to) hope, (put, make to) trust, rely on, take refuge in.

This idea of taking refuge may well derive from the common experience of fugitives or men of war, for whom the adjacent hills provided a ready "safe height" or "strong rock" to which the often helpless defender could hurry for protection. "The Lord redeemeth the soul of his servants: and none of them that trust in him shall be desolate" (Psalm 34:22). "He that dwelleth in the secret place of the most High shall abide under the shadow of the Almighty. I will say of the Lord, He is my refuge and my fortress: my God; in him will I trust" (Psalm 91:1–2). "Trust in the Lord with all thine heart; and lean not unto thine own understanding" (Proverbs 3:5).

The second key is rest. The Hebrew word for rest is "noo'-akh" (Strong's Exhaustive Concordance). It means to rest, i.e. settle down; to dwell, stay, fall, place, let alone, withdraw, give comfort, etc. KJV—cease, be confederate (to be united), lay, let down, (be) quiet, remain, (cause to, be at, give comfort, etc.). Rest signifies a fixed and secure habitation. Rest also has the following figurative meanings: to learn, or trust in, to continue fixed, to come to an end and to cease from war. The last definition is probably my favorite. Jesus says, "Come unto me, all ye that labour and are heavy laden, and I will give you rest. Take my yoke upon you, and learn of me; for I am meek and lowly in heart: and ye shall find rest unto your souls. For my yoke is easy, and my burden is light" (Matthew 11:28–30). "For we which have believed do enter into rest, as he said, As I have sworn in my wrath, if they shall enter into my rest: although the works were finished from the foundation of the world" (Hebrews 4:3). "For he that is entered into his [God's] rest, he also hath ceased from his own works, as God did from his. Let us labour therefore to enter into that rest, lest any man fall after the same example of unbelief" (Hebrews 4:10–11).

God's greatest pleasure is to be believed! When we come to the place where we have learned to rest in God, it is evidence that we believe Him to fulfill in our lives what He promises in His Word. That's why it is literally impossible to please Him if we do not believe or have faith in Him for everything! Webster's Dictionary defines "believe" as 1) to take as true, real, etc., 2) to trust a statement or promise of (a person) , 3) to suppose or think, to have faith (in).

The third key is *wait*. The Hebrew word for wait is "kaw-vaw'; a primitive root; to bind together (perhaps by twisting), i.e. collect; (figuratively) to expect: KJV—gather (together), look, patiently, tarry, wait (for, on, upon) (Strong's Exhaustive Concordance). This root means to wait or look for with great expectation. Waiting with steadfast endurance is a great expression of faith. It means enduring patiently in confident hope that God will decisively act for the salvation of His people. Those who wait in true faith are renewed in strength so that they can serve the Lord while looking for His saving work. His faith is strengthened in them through His testings of them, and His character is further developed in them.

Paul, in his letter to the believers in Rome said, "But if we hope for that we see not, then do we with patience wait for it" (Romans 8:25). There are many similar scriptures, such as the following: "But they that wait upon the Lord shall renew their strength; they shall mount up with wings as eagles; they shall run, and not be weary; and they shall walk, and not faint" (Isaiah 40:31). "For we through the Spirit wait for the hope of righteousness by faith" (Galatians 5:5). "Wait on the Lord: be of good courage, and he shall strengthen thine heart: wait, I say, on the Lord" (Psalm 27:14). "For evildoers shall be cut off: but those that wait upon the Lord, they shall inherit the earth" (Psalm 37:9). "Lead me in thy truth, and teach me: for thou art the God of my salvation; on thee do I wait all the day" (Psalm 25:5).

Can you see why the Lord said that anxious spirits are the archenemy to faith? Whenever we become so weighed down and blinded by the cares of this life, as I had, what we have in fact done is caused our relationship with God to suffer. Jesus warns us of this, "And take heed to yourselves, lest at any time your hearts be overcharged with surfeiting, and drunkenness, and cares of this life, and so that day come upon you unawares" (Luke 21:34). Anxious spirits will always attempt to hinder our faith (our ability to trust, rest, and wait) in God. If you think about it, each of these three keys that make up God-pleasing faith is terribly disrupted whenever we succumb to anxious and impatient spirits.

When we succumb to anxious spirits, we stop trusting God. Instead, we begin looking toward or relying on our own abilities or the provisions and abilities of others to fulfill the needs we may have. This is putting confidence in the flesh! "For we are the circumcision, which worship God in the spirit, and rejoice in Christ Jesus, and have no confidence in the flesh" (Philippians 3:3).

Whenever we are anxious, our ability to rest in God is disrupted! When we are anxious, our tendency is to leave the protection of God who is our fortress, with all of His benefits, and wander away from Him. Remember the old military adage, "Divide and conquer!" The enemy of our souls knows this all too well.

When we are anxious, our ability to wait on God is also hindered drastically. When we allow ourselves to be swept away by anxiousness, our tendency is to try to outrun God. When we don't get what we want when we want it, waiting is the last thing we feel like doing. So what do we do? We try to make things happen on our own. What we are doing then is telling God, "I don't believe You or Your Word!" Can you see how this would displease God? Remember, without faith it is impossible to please God! When we try to possess something before it is God's time for us to have it, we are calling down a curse on our own heads.

Anything that stands in the way of our trusting in, resting in, and waiting on God for everything in our lives displeases Him! What God truly desires for us is that we learn how to trust Him for everything in the same way that a little child knows without a doubt that he or she will have all their needs provided without fail. "And Jesus called a little child unto him, and set him in the midst of them, And said, Verily I say unto you, Except ye be converted, and become as little children, ye shall not enter into the kingdom of heaven" (Matthew 18:2–3).

It is this same kind of childlike faith in Him that God desires that we all acquire. How do we get it? We get it by first letting down the walls in our lives that have hindered us from opening ourselves up to sound Biblical counsel and investing the time necessary to get to know God and His Word in an intimate way. Remember, everything that God does is for the purpose of our being able to possess a close and deeply personal relationship with Himself, and it is our faith that bonds us together. Without faith, we are walking in sin. Paul teaches us, "Hast thou faith? have it to thyself before God. Happy is he that condemneth not himself in that thing which he alloweth. And he that doubteth is damned if he eat, because he eateth not of faith: for whatsoever is not of faith is sin" (Romans 14:22–23). We must place all of our confidence in God! This is why Paul so emphatically teaches us, "But without faith it is impossible to please him: for he that cometh to God must believe that he is, and that he is a rewarder of them that diligently seek him" (Hebrews 11:6).

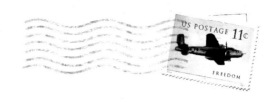

Understanding the Fear of the Lord

Through the years, I have had the privilege of speaking into the lives of hundreds of people who have come out of or are currently trapped in abusive family situations. The more time I spend with each of them, the more evident it is to me that there is a common thread which runs through the center of each of their lives. Unfortunately, the thread I am speaking of is a terribly distorted view of what a dad's role in the family is truly supposed to be. Whenever I ask any of them about their dads and what kind of relationship they have with them, nine times out of ten, the reaction is the same. Their countenance drops, they hang their heads, and they take an obviously defensive posture against anything that has to do with him.

I understand full well that moms in these same environments can be just as abusive as dads at times, but it is primarily the dad's role that I would like to focus on for this particular message. Please note that when I talk about abusive dads here I am not referring to the scoundrels who physically and mentally abuse their wives or children. I am rather addressing those who, due to the neglect of their own relationship with God and His Word, open their families up to all manner of perversion, for perversion is any lifestyle or activity that runs contrary to the wonderful fullness of a life in Christ Jesus.

> Because I have called, and ye refused; I have stretched out my hand, and no man regarded; But ye have set at nought all my counsel, and would none of my reproof: I also will laugh at your calamity; I will mock when your fear cometh; When your fear cometh as desolation, and your destruction cometh as a whirlwind; when distress and anguish cometh upon you. Then shall they call upon me, but I will not answer; they shall seek me early, but they shall not find me: For that they hated knowledge, and did not choose the fear of the LORD: They would none of my counsel: they despised all my reproof. Therefore shall they eat of the fruit of their own way, and be filled with their own devices.
> Proverbs 1:24–31

When God designed the concept of family, He did it knowing full well that in order for it to be successful, the dad must be the high priest or spiritual leader of his household. Anything less subjects the entire family, and ultimately anyone else that they come in contact with, to a life that is cursed!

Please note that by making this statement concerning dads I am in no way being critical of single moms who are raising their children in an environment where, for whatever reason, a dad is not present. If you are a single mom, please know that God stands more than ready to provide for you an extra measure of His grace to assist you in raising your child or children in just as healthy a fashion as there is in any home where a godly dad is present, as long as you seek Him diligently, uphold righteousness in your life and home, and keep your family focused on performing the Gospel that Jesus preached.

If you are an unmarried mom raising boys, God also has a wonderful way of bringing strong male figures into their lives for the purpose of imparting to them the necessary masculine influence that they need to bring a healthy balance to their character. Just be sure that the men that they are exposed to all love God as well! For example, even though I had a great dad at home growing up, I probably received the majority of the strong male influence in my own life from fifteen years of wonderful football coaches, bosses at work, and the priceless example of my pastor of more than twenty-five years. God's grace will always be sufficient for whatever we need!

And lest I should be exalted above measure through the abundance of the revelations, there was given to me a thorn in the flesh, the messenger of Satan to buffet me, lest I should be exalted above measure. For this thing I besought the Lord thrice, that it might depart from me. And he said unto me, My grace is sufficient for thee: for my strength is made perfect in weakness. Most gladly therefore will I rather glory in my infirmities, that the power of Christ may rest upon me.

2 Corinthians 12:7–9

God's wonderful grace is also available to moms who are living in family situations where a dad is in the home, but is spiritually absent. Whatever your circumstances at home might be, it is God's design for the proper operation of the family that you seek Him with all of your heart and lead your family in the direction that God tells you to lead them, despite what modern culture or Satan himself may dictate to you. Jesus teaches us, "It is written, Man shall not live by bread alone, but by every word that proceedeth out of the mouth of God" (Matthew 4:4). In other words, the principle ingredient for a successful life is not food; the principle ingredient for a successful life is hearing God's voice, being remade by it, and doing it. That calls for a life that is wholeheartedly committed to diligently seeking God. In a nutshell, that is the way that God designed and desires the family to continually operate. When dads do not have that close and personal relationship with God that allows them to hear His voice of direction for their families, they will inevitably suffer a lifeless existence right from the start. Remember, death in the eyes of God does not occur when our heart stops and we are buried six feet under the ground; death in God's eyes occurs when we are separated from Him!

Families who do not walk closely with God will suffer all manner of abuses, and ultimately that blood will be on the dad's head! It is these families being led away from God into secular humanism that are so inclined to equate success by the size of one's financial portfolio, or by one's standing in the marketplace or community. "Better is little with the fear of the Lord than great treasure and trouble therewith" (Proverbs 15:16). Now, don't get me wrong, there is nothing at all wrong with having money and a favorable name, just as long as they are both obtained in a godly fashion. "A good name is rather to be chosen than great riches, and loving favour rather than silver and gold" (Proverbs 22:1).

It is this same secular mindset in our society that so often packs up the kids and ships them off to a college to prepare to do something that God never intended for them to do in the first place, all because the dad did not invest the time and effort needed to find God's desired purpose for His children. God has a will and plan for each of us to fulfill while here on earth, and the greatest thing that a dad can ever do for his child is to help them learn how to find their way to the throne of God so that they may get His assignment for themselves. The purpose of a thing can only be found in the mind of the maker of the thing! In our case, that is God alone!

When dads do not seek God on the behalf of their children, pray over their lives, or stand firmly as an example of Christ-likeness, abuse is inevitable! Please know, anything taken or done outside of God's will and original intent for a person or a thing always falls into the category of abuse. What is abuse? Abuse is simply abnormal use! Whenever we use something in a fashion that is contrary to the original intent and purpose of the one who created it, that is abnormal use or abuse. In order to prevent abuse from occurring in each of our lives, Jesus lays out this answer for the prevention of all such things when He says,

> Abide in me, and I in you. As the branch cannot bear fruit of itself, except it abide in the vine; no more can ye, except ye abide in me. I am the vine, ye are the branches: He that abideth in me, and I in him, the same bringeth forth much fruit: for without me ye can do nothing. If a man abide not in me, he is cast forth as a branch, and is withered; and men gather them, and cast them into the fire, and they are burned. If ye abide in me, and my words abide in you, ye shall ask what ye will, and it shall be done unto you.
>
> John 15:4–7

When a dad does not live in Christ Jesus and assume his proper place as the high priest or spiritual leader of his family, not only is he disobeying God, but he is also unleashing on the members of his family unclean spirits of confusion, rejection, crippling insecurities, and many other things. This goes for unmarried moms as well!

Everything that I have written thus far has been done to make this most important point. When a child is in or has gone through an abusive family situation where the dad does not assume his God-given assignment, it is extremely difficult to help that child understand the concept of God as being a loving, just, and caring Father—no matter how old the child might be. In most cases, because they have been exposed for so long to a distorted version of God's original intent for what a father is supposed to be, they find it tremendously difficult to relate to a father as being loving and compassionate. Whenever these kids, young or old, hear the word "father" mentioned, they immediately find themselves swept away in a wave of emotion—whether anger, bitterness, fear, or a combination of each.

All they can think of at that moment is getting as far away from a father as possible. This in turn also drives them away from God. The general mind-set of these kids is "If all I get from my dad is harsh criticism, mean looks, and beatings, then I can just imagine how much worse my punishment would be if I go to God; and frankly after all I have been through already, I don't think I can handle any more pain!" So, in their quest to find any sense of fulfillment or self-worth, they tend to look for it as far away from God and His people as possible. And we all know where that can lead. Do you see why Satan invests so much time and effort in tearing apart the sacred institution of the family? "And Jesus knew their thoughts, and said unto them, Every kingdom divided against itself is brought to desolation; and every city or house divided against itself shall not stand" (Matthew 12:25).

That is not at all the kind of fear we are meant to have where our wonderful heavenly Father is concerned! Think about it for a moment, Dad or Mom. What do you think it will be like standing before an almighty and awesome God on the day of judgment to find that you as a parent did more to drive your child away from God than you ever did to lead him or her to Him, all because you raised them to know your carnal nature and fleshly fears rather than the nature of the person of almighty God? If this cycle of carnality in your own life is not broken, you will unleash a curse on your children that will wreak havoc on them, their children, and their children's children. God makes it very plain when He says,

> Thou shalt have no other gods before me. Thou shalt not make unto thee any graven image, or any likeness of any thing that is in heaven above, or that is in the earth beneath, or that is in the water under the earth: Thou shalt not bow down thyself to them, nor serve them: for I the LORD thy God am a jealous God, visiting the iniquity of the fathers upon the children unto the third and fourth generation of them that hate me.
>
> Exodus 20:3–5

Never forget, you are only your child's parent. God is their Father!

"The fear of the Lord is the beginning of knowledge" (Proverbs 1:7). What does this scripture mean? What is the fear of the Lord? Before we discuss what the fear of the Lord is, let's look at some definitions for the word "fear." Webster's Dictionary defines "fear" as 1) anxiety caused by real or possible danger, pain, etc; fright, 2) awe; reverence 3) apprehension; concern. Vine's Expository Dictionary says the Hebrew word for fear is "yare'" (pronounced yaw-ray') "to be afraid, stand in awe, fear." When used for a person in an exalted position, "yare'"connotes "standing in awe." This is not simple fear, but reverence—whereby an individual recognizes the power and position of the individual revered, and renders him proper respect.

In that sense, the word implies submission to a proper ethical relationship to God. As the angel of the Lord told Abraham: "I know that thou fearest God, seeing thou hast not withheld thy son, thine only son from me" (Genesis 22:12). The people who were delivered from Egypt saw God's great power, "feared the Lord, and believed the Lord, and His servant Moses" (Exodus 14:31). There is more involved here than mere fleshly or human fear. The people also showed proper honor (reverence) for God and stood in awe of Him and of His servant, as their song demonstrates (Exodus 15). However, after later experiencing the thunder, lightning flashes, sounds of the trumpet, and smoking mountain, they were afraid (but with fleshly or human fear) and drew back, but Moses told them not to be afraid, "for God is come to prove you, and that His fear [the fear of the Lord] may be before your faces, that you sin not" (Exodus 20:20).

Though this may sound at first like a contradiction, it's not. When Moses told them to not be afraid, he was telling them that they should not have human or fleshly fear. He was saying, however, that we should have the fear that comes from the Holy Spirit, which is the fear of God. "Wherefore, my beloved, as ye have always obeyed, not as in my presence only, but now much more in my absence, work out your own salvation with fear and trembling" (Philippians 2:12). It is of the utmost importance that we understand that "the fear of the Lord" is a gift from God and cannot be conjured up or produced by the arm of flesh. It is revealed only to those who diligently seek Him.

As wonderful a job as Vines and Websters have done in defining "fear," I, however, would like to share with you the definition that I personally derived from an encounter that I had one morning in 1985. As a result of the following testimony I have come to define the fear of the Lord as being "a personal knowledge of the all-consuming awesome power of almighty God!"

The encounter that I am talking about took place around four o'clock in the morning on September 13, 1985. That morning I experienced something that up to that point in my life I had only heard or read about, but had never witnessed for myself. It all started out as a dream that I had that was set in what appeared to be the ruins of an old stucco-style village like the kind that would have been in Jerusalem during the time that our Lord physically walked the earth. Appearing before me was the figure of a man whose face I never saw because he had his back to me the whole time and was wearing what seemed to be an oversized, full-length hooded robe. From the moment the dream began, I heard what sounded like thousands upon thousands of angels singing the song that Jack Hayford wrote, entitled "Majesty."

As I heard this chorus being sung in awesome beauty, I saw the robed man kneel down at the base of one of the stucco structures next to me. As he knelt, I leaned over his shoulder and watched him take both of his hands and reach into the wall of the structure, as if it were transparent, and pull out a toy-sized figure of a horse, and on the horse was a figure of a rider. The horse was about ten inches in length, and the rider on its back seemed to be a small, invisible man made visible only by very loosely-wrapped strips of cotton cloth that were wound around his body. As I continued looking over the shoulder of the man at the figure of the horse and its rider, the voices of what seemed to be legions upon legions of angels began to suddenly increase in even greater volume and power like a mighty rushing wind, not harsh to my ears but with an all-consuming beauty, and forced me to look straight up over my head. When I did, I saw, faster than the human eye can follow, an angel descending down on me from straight up above. Just as it seemed as if it was going to land right on top of me, it suddenly stopped and slapped the tips of its wings together about three inches from my face. With the clash of its wings together, I awoke from the dream.

I awoke to find my spirit hovering about two feet over my body, which was lying flat on its back in the bed. Shortly after, I experienced my spirit slowly settling back down into my body. Once back in my body,

I fought to get my hands over my face in hopes that it would somehow shield or protect me from seeing the angel or, God forbid, actually seeing Jesus Himself and being consumed like a Kleenex tissue in a raging bonfire. The terrifying fear was indescribable to say the very least! By this time, the power of God was so all-consuming, that I could not so much as move or speak. The only thing that I could think to do was to try to praise God, but by this point I couldn't even move my hands away from my face, still in fear of what I might see. The fear was like nothing I had ever experienced, seen, or even heard of before! It rendered me powerless to move, as if I had been turned to stone. It was only by the grace of God that I was able to cover my face with my hands. I was totally subject to whatever God wanted to do with me! It was also at that time that I learned, much better than I wanted to at that moment, just how frail our physical bodies are in the presence of God. For example, I was totally amazed that my heart didn't actually burst. It sure felt like it was going to. "Neither do men put new wine into old bottles: else the bottles break, and the wine runneth out, and the bottles perish: but they put new wine into new bottles, and both are preserved" (Matthew 9:17).

After about an hour had passed, the fear began to subside enough to where I started to regain the use of my faculties. I remember the first thing to come out of my mouth were pleas for Jesus to leave my room! Even the thought of seeing Him gripped my heart with a fear that can't be explained with mere words. As the horrifying, all-consuming fear continued to subside, I began to notice that it was now being replaced by an all-consuming peace. It also was like nothing that I had ever experienced or even heard of before. Just like the fear, the peace was indescribable. Within just a few short hours, the Lord had taken me from one extreme to the other. The peace of God that settled in my room (since there are no words that can ever come close to describing it) was "like" a dew or mist that fell on everything around me.

> Then there came again and touched me one like the appearance of a man, and he strengthened me, And said, O man greatly beloved, fear not: peace be unto thee, be strong, yea, be strong. And when he had spoken unto me, I was strengthened, and said, Let my lord speak; for thou hast strengthened me.
>
> Daniel 10:18–19

As the all-consuming peace of the Lord began to subside, I was then and only then able to sit up in my bed and begin worshipping Him. Believe me, I worshipped Him with every fiber of my being for, as best as I can recall, around three hours. I can vividly remember the muscles in my throat feeling as if they were on fire. My eyes had run out of tears after just the first thirty minutes or so, and my voice was literally worn out from singing praises. It was during that time that I realized that it is only because God enables us that we can even participate in the wonderful privilege of worshipping

His holy name! Another amazing thing I learned while in His presence was that there are literally no words that can even begin to describe Him! As a matter of fact, even the names "King of kings" and "Lord of lords" didn't come close to describing who He is. As His peace continued to settle in my room, I was only then able to ask God what was meant by the dream and what the significance was of the horse and its rider that He had shown me early in the dream.

He said, "The horse and its rider that I showed you represent Satan and his hoards of unclean spirits. The reason I showed them to you at the size that I did was to relay the insignificance and powerlessness they have against you while you are walking in Christ." Then He spoke something that left me speechless yet again. He asked me, "Remember how you were totally consumed with indescribable fear by what you thought was my presence? Do you remember how you were terrified beyond measure by what you thought was Jesus Himself standing in your room? Do you recall losing the complete use of your body to what you just knew were legions upon legions of angels? Keith, the truth is, I never did come anywhere near you; My precious Son never even stepped so much as one foot into your room; and what you thought were legions upon legions of angels was only one angel."

Not only was I once again totally amazed, but I also immediately remembered and understood fully the account in Matthew where he records what took place at the tomb just after Jesus rose from the dead. Matthew writes,

> In the end of the sabbath, as it began to dawn toward the first day of the week, came Mary Magdalene and the other Mary to see the sepulcher. And behold, there was a great earthquake: for the angel of the Lord descended from heaven, and came and rolled back the stone from the door, and sat upon it. His countenance was like lightning, and his raiment white as snow. And for fear of him the keepers did shake, and became as dead men.
>
> Matthew 28:1–4

Then the Lord said to me, "So, if you were totally consumed by the presence of just one angel, then how much greater things will I do with the legions that I have set at your side (and at the side of all who love me) to destroy the things that separate my children from me!" He then said, "All of the demons of hell ride a horse named 'Deception'!" He concluded by saying, "Get your pen and paper, and document exactly what you have both seen and heard." At that, I reached into my nightstand, grabbed my pen and notepad, and began the difficult task of trying to put into words the things I had seen and heard in the spirit. And if I might add, this brief account does in no way begin to describe the awesomeness of what had taken place.

In that brief moment of time in 1985, I received an understanding of the fear of the Lord in a way that I had never known before. It was this new understanding that enabled me to adopt as my own personal definition of the fear of the Lord as being "a personal knowledge of the all-consuming awesome power of almighty God!" Although what I experienced that morning was terrifying beyond description, I found it to be something that never turned me against or drove me away from God but rather that endeared me to Him in a profound way. I now know that the part of me that wanted to flee the presence of the glory of the Lord was my old sin nature. While my old nature was terrified, my new nature was strengthened tremendously. What took place firmly set my affections on God and established in my heart a love for Him the likes that until then I did not think was even possible. "In the fear of the Lord is strong confidence: and his children shall have a place of refuge. The fear of the Lord is a fountain of life, to depart from the snares of death" (Proverbs 14:26–27).

Unlike the damaging "fleshly fear" that is experienced by a child who is exposed to an abusive parent, experiencing the awesome presence of God, hence the fear of the Lord, establishes a reverence and awe of God which opens the doorway to understanding like nothing else can. "The fear of the LORD is the beginning of wisdom: a good understanding have all they that do his commandments: his praise endureth for ever" (Psalm 111:10).

A wise man will hear, and will increase learning; and a man of understanding shall attain unto wise counsels: to understand a proverb, and the interpretation; the words of the wise, and their dark sayings. The fear of the LORD is the beginning of knowledge: but fools despise wisdom and instruction. My son, hear the instruction of thy father, and forsake not the law of thy mother: For they shall be an ornament of grace unto thy head, and chains about thy neck.

Proverbs 1:5–9

Where the fear of the Lord is absent in the life of a Christian, lifeless religion will prevail!

But if you have never experienced anything like the things that I have shared with you in this testimony, it in no way means that God does not love you, or that He respects someone else more than He does you. "Then Peter opened his mouth, and said, Of a truth I perceive that God is no respecter of persons" (Acts 10:34). Yet though God is not a respecter of persons, He is a rewarder of those who diligently seek Him! "Be not deceived; God is not mocked: for whatsoever a man soweth, that shall he also reap" (Galatians 6:7). If you desire for the Lord to show Himself to you in a great way, then you must seek Him diligently! "But without faith it is impossible to please him: for he that cometh to God must believe that he is, and that he is a rewarder of them that diligently seek him" (Hebrews 11:6).

If you noticed, Paul did not say that God is a rewarder of them who *merely* seek Him. He said that God is a rewarder of them that *diligently* seek Him! This walk with God is an all in or all out endeavor! "I know thy works, that thou art neither cold nor hot: I would thou wert cold or hot. So then because thou art lukewarm, and neither cold nor hot, I will spue thee out of my mouth" (Revelation 3:15–16). "As many as I love, I rebuke and chasten: be zealous therefore, and repent" (Revelation 3:19). God wants nothing more than to draw close to us, but the only thing that hinders Him from doing so is our own lack of desire to first draw close to Him! "Draw nigh to God, and [then] he will draw nigh to you" (James 4:8).

The sole reason that I have shared this testimony and teaching with you is in the hope that it will create in you an unquenchable desire to seek God with your whole heart, mind, body, and soul! If you have given yourself entirely to God and have yet to experience anything like I have shared in this letter, do not be discouraged! If God so decides to reveal Himself to you in that way, He will do it in His time! It is very important, however, to also know that God can show Himself to you in many different ways. Thinking that God only shows Himself to us in the way that I experienced in my earlier testimony is a terrible misunderstanding of how He does things. As a matter of fact, perhaps some of the greatest moves of God that I have personally experienced have been when He has showed Himself big in the small matters of my life. Whether it was getting a much-needed check in the mail just as a bill came due, getting an encouraging phone call when I needed it most, or hearing His soft and gentle whisper in my spirit, God has many ways that He can reveal

Himself to each of us, ways that will build our faith like nothing else can.

I also happen to believe with all of my heart that He has an extra special reward that awaits those who diligently seek Him and walk faithfully with Him, but for whatever reason have never experienced what most might refer to as a major miracle or vision of God. For example, do you know how "doubting Thomas" got his nickname? It happened shortly after Jesus had been resurrected.

But Thomas, one of the twelve, called Didymus, was not with them when Jesus came. The other disciples therefore said unto him, We have seen the Lord. But he [Thomas] said unto them, Except I shall see in his hands the print of the nails, and put my finger into the print of the nails, and thrust my hand into his side, I will not believe.

John 20:24–25

Jesus, knowing full well Thomas' every thought, had already prepared to help him quickly become "believing Thomas," while at the same time including a powerful statement concerning those who have not experienced a great vision of Jesus but still believe on Him.

And after eight days again his disciples were within, and Thomas with them: then came Jesus, the doors being shut, and stood in the midst, and said, Peace be unto you. Then saith he to Thomas, Reach hither thy finger, and behold my hands; and reach hither thy hand, and thrust it into my side: and be not faithless, but believing. And Thomas answered and said unto him, My Lord and my God. Jesus saith unto him, Thomas, because thou hast seen me, thou hast believed: blessed are they that have not seen, and yet have believed.

John 20:26–29

I pray that this letter has helped you better understand the fear of the Lord, and has filled you with the unquenchable desire to remove all distractions from your life and seek God with your whole heart! I also pray that you will make His presence your permanent residence and will give your life to leading those around you into a close and intimate relationship with our almighty God and King—the kind of intimate relationship that will enable them to continually experience the wonderful fear of the Lord!

Give to Give

If you were to walk straight out the back door of my house, over the railroad tracks, and about an eighth of a mile through the woods, you would find yourself on the campus of Warwick High School, the alma mater of former star NFL quarterback Michael Vick. Early on it became obvious to everyone in town that this gifted young athlete was developing an almost Michael Jordan kind of athletic quality, and we all knew that great things were in store for him. As a senior at Warwick, Michael was scouted by the top universities around the country, but he chose to stay close to home and signed with Virginia Tech. Each year that he played established him even more in the eyes of pro scouts as an extremely valuable commodity. When he became eligible for the NFL draft, team owners and coaches all over the league began frantically moving players and draft picks around like pieces on a board game in hopes of positioning themselves for a shot at acquiring Michael's talents. He was initially drafted by the San Diego Chargers, but he waived their offer and signed with the Falcons. It was a big day for Atlanta, to say the least, when the Falcons signed Michael. John Madden, the popular sports commentator, said on numerous occasions that Michael Vick brought a whole new level of excitement to the game of football and was the most gifted player that he has ever watched play. What a rare and valuable find!

Just as NFL scouts are continuously looking for extra special players like Michael, God is also always searching far and wide to find extra special standouts where obedience to His Word is concerned. "For the ways of man are before the eyes of the Lord, and he pondereth all his goings" (Proverbs 5:21). When He finds such a person, it thrills His heart beyond measure! Why? Because God loves to give, and in order for a giver to be able to give, they must first have a qualified receiver. Without a qualified receiver, a giver is miserable! This is a matter of the heart, because, as in the case of Michael Vick, appearances can be deceiving. That is why it is of the utmost importance that we are not only hearers of God's Word but are continuously doing His Word. "Wherefore lay apart all filthiness and superfluity of naughtiness, and receive with meekness the engrafted word, which is able to save your souls. But be ye doers of the word, and not hearers only, deceiving your own selves" (James 1:21–22). Remember, only those who truly love, believe, and obey God's Word qualify to receive His rewards!

Down through the years, I have noticed that perhaps the one area where God is not believed most often is in the area of giving. I am not saying that people are not giving at all or that all those who do give have selfish ulterior motives. I am saying that I believe that the vast majority who are giving in the church today are doing so with strings attached. Some give to silence something deep within themselves, others to obtain money, houses, cars, relationships, jobs, favor, position, etc. At any rate, the general consensus can be stated thusly: if there is nothing in it for me, why "throw away" my hard-earned money, especially if it means running the risk of never receiving a return on it? Believe me, anyone who thinks this way does not really know God! Although this marketplace frame of thought may serve well on Wall Street, it has no place in the body of Christ! "For we [true believers] walk by faith, not by sight" (2 Corinthians 5:7).

Just what is at the root of this self-centered way of thinking? In large part, this mindset has been forged at the hands of those teaching an unbalanced version of what the scriptures teach us about God's process of seed, time, and harvest. This misrepresentation of God's original intent for the process of sowing and reaping has instilled into the hearts and minds of those who practice it a "buy a miracle" mentality. This destroys in them everything that Jesus teaches us about storing up for ourselves treasures in heaven.

> Lay not up for yourselves treasures upon earth, where moth and rust doth corrupt, and where thieves break through and steal: but lay up for yourselves treasures in heaven, where neither moth nor rust doth corrupt,

and where thieves do not break through nor steal: for where your treasure is, there will your heart be also.

Matthew 6:19–21

If you have lived in the United States for any length of time at all, you know that this is a nation where materialism reigns supreme. If we Christians are not well-educated concerning godly giving, we too can find ourselves deceived into offering up our money, goods, and services for the wrong reasons. We will be giving not for the purpose of the glorification or the pure worship of God, but in exchange for what amounts to no more than playing the lottery, i.e. giving in the hope that one day we will "hit the jackpot." However, when we put man's teachings above God's, we are asking for trouble. "My people are destroyed for lack of knowledge: because thou hast rejected knowledge, I will also reject thee, that thou shalt be no priest to me: seeing thou hast forgotten the law of thy God, I will also forget thy children" (Hosea 4:6). I am not saying that God does not bless us with a harvest for seed sown in fertile soil. After all, everything God does is based on seed, time, and harvest. I am saying that it is time that we thoroughly examine our heart's motives for why we are sowing to begin with. "Ye ask, and receive not, because ye ask amiss, that ye may consume it upon your lusts" (James 4:3). Never give to get; give to give!

Perhaps one of the most manipulatively-wielded scriptures in the quest for getting has been the following one in Luke. Jesus said, "Give, and it shall be given unto you; good measure, pressed down, and shaken together, and running over, shall men give into your bosom. For with the same measure that ye mete withal it shall be measured to you again" (Luke 6:38). I believe that this scripture, among other things, has been abused terribly for the purpose of leveraging fundraising campaigns in the church. Contrary to popular belief, Jesus is not even talking about the acquisition of money or material possessions here. If we look at just seven verses before the Luke 6:38 scripture, we will find exactly what He was talking about.

And as ye would that men should do to you, do ye also to them likewise. For if ye love them which love you, what thank have ye? For sinners also love those that love them. And if ye do good to them which do good to you, what thank have ye? For sinners also do even the same. And if ye lend to them of whom ye hope to receive, what thank have ye? For sinners also lend to sinners, to receive as much again. But love ye your enemies, and do good, and lend, hoping for nothing again; and your reward shall be great, and ye shall be the children of the Highest: for he is kind unto the unthankful and to the evil. Be ye therefore merciful, as your Father also is merciful. Judge not, and ye shall not be judged: condemn not, and ye shall not be condemned: forgive, and ye shall be forgiven.

Luke 6:31–37

Now let's read Luke 6:38 again: "Give, and it shall be given unto you; good measure, pressed down, and shaken together, and running over, shall men give into your bosom. For with the same measure that ye mete withal it shall be measured to you again." If you truly want to know what God means in scripture, it is necessary to read verses in context! What is Jesus referring to when He says "give" in this text? Is He talking primarily about money or things? No! Although one might at first glance see why so many have misused this scripture to teach sowing and reaping for the purpose of material or monetary gain, if we look at it in context with the previous verses, it becomes obvious that Jesus was actually talking about the way we should treat one another. He states in Luke 6:35, "But love ye your enemies, and do good, and lend, hoping for nothing again; and your reward shall be great, and ye shall be the children of the Highest."

Before we can ever expect to receive anything from God, we must first learn how to give love and goodness to others, *hoping for nothing again* as Jesus instructs us. This is the key! Do you realize that Jesus, just by making this one statement, is knowingly safeguarding us from the tormenting wrath of unreal or unreasonable expectations? I am convinced these expectations are the primary cause of depression in the lives of millions of people today. When we give to get, we are setting ourselves up for all manner of disappointing frustration. "And if ye lend to them of whom ye hope to receive, what thank have ye? For sinners also lend to sinners, to receive as much again" (Luke 6:34).

In order for us to walk in the promise that Jesus is making here, we must first come to know beyond a shadow of a doubt that our provider is God alone and not our employers, parents, friends, or anyone else! If we don't know this wholeheartedly, what we tend to do is show an impure form of love and goodness toward God and others, in the hope of their giving to us in return. Not only is this the practice of manipulation, a form of witchcraft, but it disqualifies those who do practice it from receiving all that God has for them. In short, what we are doing is giving up everything that God has to offer to possess very little at best. Remember, God can do in one second what it can take a million people a lifetime to accomplish.

If we give love and goodness to others with a pure heart, "hoping for nothing again," then we are freeing up God to move on others to meet whatever need we may have when we need it. Prosperity is not having everything, prosperity is having exactly what you need, when you need it! "Beloved, I wish above all things that thou mayest prosper and be in health, even as thy soul prospereth" (3 John 1:2). How does our soul prosper?

Blessed is the man that walketh not in the counsel of the ungodly, nor standeth in the way of sinners, nor sitteth in the seat of the scornful. But his delight is in the law of the LORD; and in his law doth he meditate day and night. And he shall be like a tree planted by the rivers of water, that bringeth forth his fruit in his season; his leaf also shall not wither; and whatsoever he doeth shall prosper.

Psalm 1:1–3

This is true prosperity!

Because of a total misunderstanding of what prosperity truly is, many in the Church are pursuing material gain. Many think and even teach that material gain is synonymous with God's definition of prosperity. This could not be further from the truth.

And they that have believing masters, let them not despise them, because they are brethren; but rather do them service, because they are faithful and beloved, partakers of the benefit. These things teach and exhort. If any man teach otherwise, and consent not to wholesome words, even the words of our Lord Jesus Christ, and to the doctrine which is according to godliness; He is proud, knowing nothing, but doting about questions and strifes of words, whereof cometh envy, strife, railings, evil surmisings, Perverse disputings of men of corrupt minds, and destitute of the truth, supposing that gain is godliness: from such withdraw thyself. But godliness with contentment is great gain.

1 Timothy 6:2–6

The notion that gain is godliness is, in fact, an unbalanced version of the true prosperity message. Material prosperity was never intended by God to be something that we should pursue. Our passion is to be for the pursuit of God and Him alone! Once we get this firmly fixed in our hearts and minds, then true prosperity can begin to flow from the hand of God into our lives and not a second before. Godly prosperity is a result of diligently seeking God first! Jesus said,

> And why take ye thought for raiment? Consider the lilies of the field, how they grow; they toil not, neither do they spin: And yet I say unto you, That even Solomon in all his glory was not arrayed like one of these. Wherefore, if God so clothe the grass of the field, which to day is, and to morrow is cast into the oven, shall he not much more clothe you, O ye of little faith? Therefore take no thought, saying, What shall we eat? or, What shall we drink? or, Wherewithal shall we be clothed? (For after all these things do the Gentiles seek) for your heavenly Father knoweth that ye have need of all these things. But seek ye first the kingdom of God, and his righteousness; and all these things shall be added unto you.
>
> Matthew 6:28–33

Joshua when exhorting the Reubenites, the Gadites, and the half tribe of Manasseh said,

> But take diligent heed to do the commandment and the law, which Moses the servant of the LORD charged you, to love the Lord your God, and to walk in all his

ways, and to keep his commandments, and to cleave unto him, and to serve him with all your heart and with all your soul.

Joshua 22:5

This and only this is the birthplace of true prosperity!

Now, let's take a look again at Luke 6:38 in the light of what I have shared thus far. "Give, and it shall be given unto you; good measure, pressed down, and shaken together, and running over, shall men give into your bosom." If you noticed, Jesus did not say that men shall give into your treasury, stables, or storehouse. He said they shall give into your bosom. What is meant by the word bosom here? Webster's Dictionary defines "bosom" as 1) the human breast, 2) the breast regarded as the source of feelings, 3) the interior midst. Noah Webster's 1828 edition defines "bosom," as

in composition, implies intimacy, affection and confidence; as a bosom friend, an intimate or confidential friend; bosom-lover, bosom-interest, bosom-secret. In such phrases, bosom may be considered as an attribute equivalent to intimate, confidential, dear.

Now, let's read this again. "Give, and it shall be given unto you; good measure, pressed down, and shaken together, and running over, shall men give into your bosom" (Luke 6:38). If with a pure motive you give to give, "hoping for nothing again," God can then move on the hearts of others to give to you, compounded, the love and kindness that you have given to others. I am in no way stating that we will necessarily receive back from the same person or persons that we have given kindness to or that we will receive what we want when we think we need it. I am saying that God will see to it that we will, in His time, in His way, and through those He chooses, receive a harvest of love and kindness into our own bosom or heart. We must come to the place in our lives where we totally trust, rest, and wait on God! Don't be deceived, our heavenly Father always knows what's best for us! Despite how discouraged we may become with the moral state of those around us in the world today, we must not let anything hinder us from continually giving for the sake of giving alone!

> Be not deceived; God is not mocked: for whatsoever a man soweth, that shall he also reap. For he that soweth to his flesh shall of the flesh reap corruption; but he that soweth to the Spirit shall of the Spirit reap life everlasting. And let us not be weary in well doing: for in due season we shall reap, if we faint not. As we have therefore opportunity, let us do good unto all men, especially unto them who are of the household of faith.
>
> Galatians 6:7–10

Paul teaches in this verse something that I know that none of us really likes to hear, that tormenting little phrase "in due season." Why don't most of us like hearing this? Because it implies waiting to receive our promise for an undisclosed period of time. In this day and time, waiting is not popular or very well received. However, waiting is necessary if we are to receive the promises of God. "And let us not be weary in well doing: for in due season we shall reap, if we faint not" (Galatians 6:9). What would cause us to faint? A lack of believing that God will do exactly as He has promised in His Word!

Here is how it works. Unbelief produces fleshly fear. Fear leads to doubt. Doubt leads to striving. Striving produces fatigue. Fatigue gives way to faintheartedness. So, if failing to believe God ultimately causes us to become faint of heart, then it would stand to reason that believing God will prevent us from becoming fainthearted.

> Abide in me, and I in you. As the branch cannot bear fruit of itself, except it abide in the vine; no more can ye, except ye abide in me. I am the vine, ye are the branches: He that abideth in me, and I in him, the same bringeth forth much fruit: for without me ye can do nothing.
>
> John 15:4–5

This includes giving the right way! Without an understanding of God's heart for giving, all we can do is abuse it! So, give love, encouragement, and kindness from a pure heart, "and it shall be given unto you; good measure, pressed down, and shaken together, and running over, shall men give into your bosom. For with the same measure that ye mete withal it shall be measured to you again" (Luke 6:38). "Therefore all things whatsoever ye would that men should do to you, do ye even so to them: for this is the law and the prophets" (Matthew 7:12) Jesus says, "A new commandment I give unto you, That ye love one another; as I have loved you, that ye also love one another. By this shall all men know that ye are my disciples, if ye have love one to another" (John 13:34–35). Always give to give!

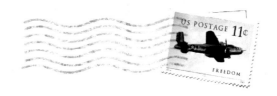

The Prayer of Salvation

Father God, in the precious name of Jesus Christ, the King of kings and the Lord of all lords, I lay my life at your feet. I come before you confessing that I am a sinner, and am asking that you forgive me of all my sins, those that I know that I have committed as well as those that I am not even aware of. I ask that you come into my heart and be my Lord. I lay my life and everything in it at your feet, and ask that you would take me now and begin the process of changing me into your likeness. I ask that you redeem the time that has past and allow me the opportunity to become exactly what you have predestined me to be from the foundation of the earth. I commit my life to you now, and thank you for receiving me as your own. In the wonderful name of Jesus Christ, the son of the living God, Amen.

Welcome Home!

If you have just prayed this prayer we want to congratulate you for making the greatest decision you can ever make. By accepting Jesus Christ as your personal Lord and Savior, you have begun the wonderful process of being grafted into the family of God, and we welcome you home. We would like to invite you to contact us so that we can send you information that will help you begin your new relationship with God. We advise that you begin fellowshipping with Holy Spirit-filled, Bible-believing Christians right away. We advise that you begin reading your Bible daily, whether you understand it or not. Always remember, God is not nearly as consumed with your understanding Him as He is with your believing Him! The Bible is like no other book that has ever been written, for it is literally alive and has the ability to—as you read it—become stored in your heart where the Holy Spirit can bring to your remembrance the scriptures that are applicable to whatever you are going through at any time. Be prepared, the transformation process that you have now begun will be difficult at times, and you will be tempted to go back to your old way of living. It is at times like these that hangin' out with strong Christian friends and mentors is of the utmost importance. There really is strength in numbers! Again, welcome to the family of God!

Special Heartfelt Thanks to the Team:

Bennie Nelson
"Dr." Philip Nelson
Carol Wieseman
Debby White
Dr. Ella Spry
Paul Boggs
and all of our faithful partners without whose self-less generosity this book could not have been possible.

When you have finished reading
this book, would you please
consider helping us spread this
very important and timely message
by passing it along to a friend?
Thank you!

Please keep in touch!

Eagle Project Communications
Post Office Box 1152
Yorktown, Virginia 23692
www.towardthemark.com

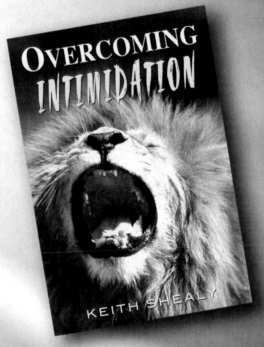

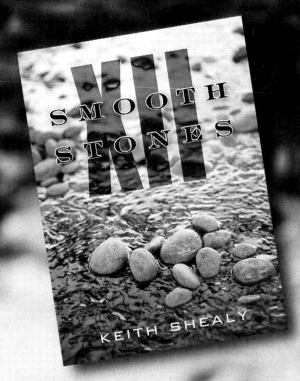

POWERFUL MUSIC!

"Between The Lines" is a collection of ten of Keith's original compositions along with one song written by Scott Allen entitled "Won By One." This project has been a long time in the making and we all have great expectation of what the songs will do to reach the lost and strengthen believers all around the world.

"Keith Shealy's new CD, "Between The Lines," is without a doubt one of the freshest, most full-of-life-and truth recordings I have ever heard! "Between The Lines" feels like an invigorating shower of God's love!"

Len Mink

www.towardthemark.com

Other Life Changing Resources

Keith and the team of Toward The Mark are also continually working to provide the Christian community with many other valuable resources like their Monthly Teaching Letters, Newsletters, T-shirts & Stickers that preach and so much more.